D1272152

The Adventures of a Treasure Hunter

CHARLES P. EVERITT

The Adventures of a Treasure Hunter

A Rare Bookman in Search of American History

by
CHARLES P. EVERITT

Little, Brown and Company · *Boston* · 1951

FIRST EDITION

Published simultaneously
in Canada by McClelland and Stewart Limited

PRINTED IN THE UNITED STATES OF AMERICA

For my wife, Elizabeth

Publisher's Note

The manuscript of these professional adventures of the late Charles P. Everitt was finished and delivered to his publisher before Mr. Everitt's death on March 4, 1951. The final script had the benefit of the author's corrections and revisions. The one missing portion of the manuscript as planned by Mr. Everitt was an Acknowledgment in which he intended to express his appreciation to those who had helped him in the preparation of his book. These are Mr. Barrows Mussey, Jr., who, as editor and friend, participated extensively in the preparation of the manuscript; Mr. Michael J. Walsh, who read the finished script with the eye of a friend and a fellow bookman; all of the bookmen, scholars and collectors whose friendships Charles P. Everitt found so rewarding and whose experiences and adventures help make up the body of this book; and his wife, Elizabeth Thompson Everitt, to whom the book is dedicated.

The Adventures of a Treasure Hunter

PART I

Americana — What and So What?

THE LAST Saturday afternoon of September, 1890, at seventeen years of age, I was up in a haymow in Scarsdale, New York, forking away the hay as my father pitched it up to me. It had been a bad day. When I came out of the haymow, I said to my father, "I'll milk my stint of eight cows tomorrow morning, and after that I'm finished. I'll never milk another cow nor pull another weed."

As was always his way, he said that was fine with him.

After services at the Methodist church Sunday morning, I asked the minister if he could find me a job.

The very next day he took me down to New York, and introduced me to Wilbur Ketcham, in Cooper Union, who dealt exclusively in religious books. At that particular time it made no difference to me whether it was a grocery store or a bookstore. At first the work was pretty much the same, too. Ketcham paid me five dollars a week for lugging in any books he bought and lugging away others he had sold, plus twenty-five cents if I worked until 9 P.M. One of his standard fast-moving items was the ninth edition of the *Encyclopaedia*

Britannica, in twenty-five quarto volumes. He had a rule that within eight blocks I could walk or pay my own transportation. Beyond that radius he paid my carfare one way.

One of my almost daily calls (no carfare) was a bookbindery run by an old German over east of Third Avenue. One day the binder shoved a tattered bundle of old almanacs at me.

"Somebody left these here so long ago I have no idea who it was," he said. "Give me a dollar for them."

I happened to have a dollar on me, and I handed it over.

My boss told me with considerable severity that I was hired as an office boy, not a buyer; but he finally returned my dollar.

A few days later Bishop John F. Hurst, the great collector of Americana, was in the store, and the boss (as I later heard from his secretary) improved the opportunity to sell the almanacs. They were *Poor Richard's Almanacks,* and Ketcham felt pretty cute to get $250 for them. (He did not live to see the same almanacs fetch $3200 at Bishop Hurst's auction.) As you may imagine, I was left wondering how long this had been going on. I started reading catalogues and everything else about the subject that I could lay hands on. Then a customer of Ketcham's – I wish I could remember his name – advised me to read volume one of Justin Winsor's *Narrative and Critical History of America.* That was, and is today, the best reference book relating to the discovery and early exploration of America.

As I read Winsor, I stacked him up against all the catalogues I could find. Little by little I discovered that the books in his bibliographies were ones that you never see. I doubt whether I have handled a dozen of those titles in sixty years. But I did make a beginning at learning what to look for.

In October, 1891, at the end of a year's service, I found six dollars in my Friday pay envelope. My boss (being a clergyman's son) had taught me how to swear, so I walked in and said, "What the hell does this mean?"

He asked if I didn't want my salary raised.

I said yes I did, to twenty-five dollars a week.

"Get the hell out of my office," observed Mr. Ketcham.

I asked him if he wanted two weeks' notice, and he answered yes.

Two minutes later he was down at my desk, flinging down two five-dollar bills. "Get the hell out of this place," was his parting benediction.

Next day I went to Summerfield MacLean, who was a bookseller next door to Ketcham's. "Mac," I said, "how about hiring me for twenty-five dollars a week?"

"Sure," he said. "Come in Monday."

On Sunday Mr. Ketcham drove over with a team of horses from Yonkers to Scarsdale. He said he thought he had been a little bit hasty, and would be glad to give me twenty-five dollars a week. When I told him I already had a job, he smiled and said, "Well, I'm wrong again." He was my friend for the rest of his life, something for which I have always been extremely grateful.

Americana is a word that has been thrown around very freely and very carelessly in the last twenty years, so that it may mean the Mayflower Compact or a hoop skirt or a whisky label or just nothing in particular.

When I first devoted my life to the subject, fifty odd years ago, Americana was the name for a restricted class of rarities dealt in by a few slightly eccentric booksellers. Even fewer and even more eccentric dealers were gathering American furniture by the wagonload; Currier & Ives prints were still things the cook might be forgiven for admiring.

In passing through the first half of this century I have finally reached a definition of Americana that seems all right to me. At any rate it will tell you – partly – what this book is about.

Americana means to me anything showing how and why people came here, and how they lived after they got here. In booksellers' catalogues it generally covers printed material alone, but I see no reason for any such limitation.

For instance, in 1922, when I appraised the contents of the office of Henry Bacon, the man who designed the Lincoln Memorial in Washington, I found in one portfolio a letter from Royal Cortissoz, written at 3 A.M. of a morning when the entire committee were busy trying to find the right inscription for the Lincoln Memorial. The letter read:

> DEAR HENRY:
>
> I couldn't sleep last night and at three A.M. I wrote out the following words, hoping you would find them suitable:
>
> IN THIS TEMPLE
> AS IN THE HEARTS OF THE PEOPLE
> FOR WHOM HE SAVED THE UNION
> THE MEMORY OF ABRAHAM LINCOLN
> IS ENSHRINED FOREVER

In the same portfolio was a note from President Taft, who was chairman of the committee. He suggested a change of one word in the inscription. Still in the same portfolio was a second note from Mr. Taft: "I completely fail to understand how I thought I could improve on a perfect thing."

In other portfolios were a number of letters from Abraham Lincoln's son Robert to Bacon, describing his father's ears, nose, and chin, with sketches. I saw all this material where it still is, in the Henry Bacon Room at Wesleyan University in Middletown, Connecticut. Cortissoz's note, hardly more than a scrap of paper, I consider the most inspiring bit of Lincolniana I have ever seen — although I have been quite carefully through many large collections of Lincoln letters and documents.

If you do not agree with me that this is Americana at its best, remember that no other inscription in this country, with the possible exception of that on the New York Post Office, has been seen and reverently studied by so many Americans.

I have long thought — and the opinion of historians seems to be coming my way now — that a book like old William Livingston's volume on how to raise sheep had more influence on American life than such a supreme and famous rarity as George Washington's diary of his Western trip. You can buy a copy of the Livingston without much trouble for $7.50, but you would have great difficulty in finding someone to take your $7500 for a Washington diary.

I have made a life, a living, and a hobby out of discovering and selling rare, expensive Americana, but honesty forces me to tell you that some of the most interesting and most important books in the field of Americana can still be had by anyone with a dollar and enough sense to go looking for them.

For instance, there is no more vivid picture of the real South before the Civil War than Fanny Kemble's *Life on a Georgia Plantation,* which is still a very common book.

I will say flatly that the best picture by far of American social life before the Revolution is Mrs. Grant's *Memoirs of an American Lady.*

Walter Edmonds has written nothing that compares in excitement and sustained interest with Mrs. Grant's story of life on the Schuyler Manor near Albany. And her book is so plentiful that I have had to give copies away to my friends in order to convince them of its merits.

But not all good Americana is that plentiful. Some of it in fact is not only excessively rare but actually is "discovered" in the most unusual and outlandish fashions. Sometimes the rarest item is found among worthless junk, in bundles, as odd lot batches of books and pamphlets sold at auctions are known to the trade.

Certainly one of the most famous bundles that ever existed was one bought by Dauber & Pine when I was working there in 1926. Or at least the discovery was made in that year. God knows how long the bundle had been around. The great authority on that episode is Mr. Dauber himself who tells the story as follows:

> Whenever books or collections or pamphlets turned up in the various auction rooms, it had been our practice to examine them individually; but when they were tied up in bundles or large containers so as to prevent close inspection, we just followed our flair and gambled heavily to buy them.
>
> Frequently, as soon as the material was looked over on our premises, we found it of no value and discarded it. At other times we picked out the most important pamphlets at once, and just accumulated the minor stuff.
>
> One evening in 1926, I knocked over a pile of these pamphlets, gathering dust for years and coming from heavens knows what sources, and as I stooped to pick them up, there fell out of another, contemporary but valueless, pamphlet, wherein it must have lain for years, the famous item!
>
> I recognized it at once and the next morning I put it on Mr. Everitt's desk.

It was the grandfather of all detective stories, Edgar Allan Poe's *Murders in the Rue Morgue.* Perhaps four or five copies now exist in the world. The pamphlet was originally an offprint from a magazine, made up as a salesmen's sample in an edition of possibly fifty or sixty, and the salesmen had not been able to get any orders.

I picked up my pencil and lightly marked our price on the corner: $25,000.

Mrs. Gertrude Hills, another of Mr. Dauber's associates at the time, wrote a note that brought Owen D. Young promptly to the store. He had come straight from the Morgan Library, where he had been looking at Mr. Morgan's copy of the *Murders.* The Morgan copy, the only one ever recorded at auction, had brought $3900. But it lacks the back cover.

"Nice book you've got there, Everitt," said Mr. Young.

"I thought so," I said.

"I'd like to show this to Mrs. Young," he said.

"Put it in your pocket," said I. That was on a Saturday; Monday he telephoned that this was the nicest book he had ever bought. A few days later came a check for $25,000. That copy is now in the New York Public Library, one of the great prizes in one of the world's great collections.

I might have had a hand in the selling of the Morgan copy of the *Murders in the Rue Morgue,* too, if I had not thought it imprudent. Up around Amenia, New York, there was a book scout and antique picker whom I knew, Louis Cole. One day just before closing time he came into my store on 23rd Street, and showed me the first copy of the *Murders* I ever saw.

"I want two dollars for this," he said.

Buying stuff like that is always risky, particularly from a person who might not remember our transaction later. I said,

"I'll give you your two dollars, but you come back tomorrow morning and I'll give you a lot more money."

He was most indignant. "I don't want any goddamned charity. I want two dollars," he said, and left the store.

At that time there was a certain secondhand bookstore that stayed open evenings. Cole somehow made his way over there and apparently thought he had concluded the sale for two dollars without any insulting offer of more money. A few days later the *New York Times* ran a note that Frank J. Maier, the great Poe collector, had bought a copy of the *Murders in the Rue Morgue* for $1250. This would have been a record-breaking price except that no other copy had ever been discovered to set a record. Someone showed Cole the *Times,* and the upshot, after some backing and filling, was that Cole got another $625 out of the affair.

Cole used to take me with him to auctions around Amenia, and once he called me up and said he had arranged an appointment for me to see and, if possible, buy the famous library of Benson John Lossing, the wood engraver, illustrator, and American historian. Lossing had put up a fireproof building at Dover Plains, New York, to house the library.

Lossing's heirs, his two sons, had not followed in their father's interests and knew little about books. Anyway, they showed me around the library, and I started taking samplings here and there. George Washington's will, signed in his own hand, was simply slipped into the front of a copy of Lossing's *Mount Vernon.* I tripped over one stack of books, and picked off the floor a nice little duodecimo that proved, on inspection, to be the second edition of the *Bay Psalm Book.* It so happened that Wilberforce Eames, down in the bowels of the New York Public Library, had showed me another copy only a few days before, remarking that he didn't know what this would fetch at auction but that it was rarer than the first edition. (The last sale price of the first edition that I happen to remember was $151,000.) The two heirs wanted to sell me the lot for $8000.

Cole, at my elbow, could hardly restrain his impatience. "Go on, what are you waiting for? It's cheap enough," he kept saying. I had trouble shutting him up.

"Oh, I don't know," I said. "Let's go down to Dover Plains."

First, I stopped in at the general store. "Did you know a local man named Lossing?" I asked.

"Sure, knew him well," said the storekeeper.

"I hear he had a bunch of old books," I said. "Are they any good?"

"I certainly hope so," said the merchant. "I have a chattel mortgage on them."

At the grocery and the butcher's the story was the same.

"This is no place for a minister's son," said I, misleadingly. And I went back to the wicked city without disturbing the Lossing library.

My first call was on Arthur Swann, then of the Anderson Galleries. Ultimately the library was prepared for sale by the Galleries, for which they made an elaborate catalogue.

Promptly the Library of Congress, the state of Virginia, and heaven knows how many other public authorities, wrote in to say that they had loaned such items as George Washington's will to the deceased historian, and please could they have their property back.

Even after every questioned item had been returned to its claimant, the remainder sold for more than $50,000.

Lossing was not alone among historians in borrowing unique

material and then being unable to remember where it had come from. The heirs, of course, had no way of knowing about chattel mortgages or the actual ownership of some of the items.

I remember once I had a chance to buy the library of the leading historian in an Eastern state, which I knew was full of priceless things.

On my way to inspect the books, I asked one of my friends and competitors in a neighboring city whether he had been down to see the library.

He said he had.

"What did you offer them?" I asked.

"Eleven thousand dollars."

A scout friend and I put in four days going over the library, which contained rarities that would make your hair curl. I had a very strong feeling that the executor was uneasy, and I finally concluded that getting the books out of the state was an important consideration in the sale.

I suppose that was why I succeeded in buying the library for $6500. One of the courtesies of the trade is that when a man reveals his bid on a lot you are both after, the successful buyer kicks in 10 per cent. I sent my friend a check for $650, and still had a few dollars' profit left over.

Louis Cole's boon companion, best customer, and fellow souse was an omnivorous collector named Frederick J. Skiff. For some reason or other both of them simultaneously decided to change their mode of life, give up liquor, and go west. They wound up in Portland, Oregon, where Skiff became treasurer of the department store of Olds, Wortman & King. Cole was soon a very successful book- and print-seller. You have probably read Skiff's *Adventures in Americana*, a book describing many of his scouting expeditions. I was with him on a good many of these trips, and you may care to know that his book is not only one of the most delightful volumes about collecting but it is truthful as well.

Skiff was always writing to me, boasting about his eighty-acre island in a lake in the Cascade Mountains. My wife and I found ourselves in the Thousand Islands, trying to fish and getting exceedingly bored. I said I guessed I would try the fishing in Oregon, and she decided on the White Mountains. Skiff collected not merely books and prints but pistols, silver, Northwest Indian antiquities, bedspreads, Indian baskets, and colonial furniture. His library, quite aside from the marvelous lot of Western manuscripts, contained over fifteen thousand presentation copies of contemporary authors.

You may remember that Kipling's *From Sea to Sea* described some of his experiences in Portland. These experiences did not include the fact that he tried to abolish alcohol in Portland by personal action, in the company of a lady about whom I know nothing except that she must have been a delightful companion. Fred Skiff came home one day with a bundle of forty-one books that Kipling had presented to the lady, quite indiscriminately—first editions, reprints, anything that came to hand. Each volume was inscribed in a fluttering and largely unrecognizable hand that later caused me much trouble, but luckily there was also a letter saying, "Dear ——: I want you to have these books," followed by his more or less recognizable signature.

Fred sold me the forty-one books for $500, which was only a fraction of their value in my eyes. (After two years' negotiation, I succeeded in driving the final sale price to my customer up to $150.)

You may think it funny that a collector like Fred would sell his prizes. The explanation was simple: he was so avid that he could never resist selling one lot in order to buy something else.

One morning he told me he guessed he would get rid of his collection of Northwest Americana.

I said, "I'll buy them, on one condition: I'll put a price on each volume, and you aren't to look at a single one. Neither you nor I have seven months to spend on this job."

So I would pick out a Meares's *Voyages* and say, "Forty dollars."

"What's that?" Fred would ask.

"None of your damn business," I would reply, laying the book face down out of his reach.

In this way I arrived at a figure of $5000, for which I gave a check. Not long afterward his son wrote: "You know what dad did with that money? He spent it to buy $5200 worth of other books."

He was, as I said before, connected with the Olds, Wortman & King department store. I had known Mr. Wortman for a good many years; he had formed a really important collection of primary Western travels, and he occupied a most respected position among Western collectors.

During my stay in Portland he asked me if I could have lunch with him, alone. At lunch he said, "Everitt, Mr. Olds is going to have a dinner party for you and Skiff and a few others, and I just wanted to tell you one thing. Please don't laugh at Olds's library."

As a matter of fact, I already knew Mr. Olds's reputation for buying anything between covers so long as it was expensively bound and came in more than one volume.

The dinner was absolutely delightful. We ate, drank, and talked until late in the evening, and then adjourned to the library, a room fully twenty by sixty, completely lined with books, every single one in full levant binding. I happened to notice, for instance, seven sets of Dickens, all in levant.

About one-thirty I said, "I'm pretty well worn out; I've got to go home."

This was the signal for a general exodus. As the guests were getting their coats, Mr. Olds took me into a corner.

"Everitt," he said, "I want to thank you very much for not laughing at my library. This is the story. I came west across the plains with my father when I was eleven or twelve. At one of the abandoned camps we stopped at, I found a defective copy of *David Copperfield.*

"I read it, and reread it, and reread it. I had daydreams, as any kid does, and I would tell myself that if I ever had enough money, I was going to buy all the books I wanted. Now, whenever a salesman calls with a set, the only question I ask is, 'Where do I sign?' "

Mr. Olds died not long after, willing his estate to his nephew, an army officer. The executors wrote to ask whether I could come west and appraise the library, and inquired what I would charge.

I wrote back: "I don't need to come west, and there will be no charge. The books are worth $25,000."

The executors were outraged. "Why," they wrote back, "we have receipted bills for $650,000."

I replied in a one-line note: "The books are worth $25,000."

The upshot was that the library was sold, and brought in $24,500, less commission; but the satisfaction Olds had already had from his collection would have been dirt cheap at a million dollars. I call that a happy ending to a collecting story.

During my stay in Portland Fred and I went around to a few junk shops (junk shops is the word). In one of them I did happen on two copies of a guide to Montana. It was the first book written and illustrated by Charlie Russell, the great Western illustrator. They were marked five cents each. At the time I did not feel that I got any more than a rare bookseller regards as his money's worth, because the craze for collecting Charlie Russell had barely begun. Anyhow, I took the books back east with me.

They were lying on my desk one day when I had a visitor, Dr. Philip Cole, whose medical discoveries had supplied him with the wherewithal for an estate at Lake Placid and the best Remington and Russell collection in existence. (Another one of my collector friends paid the doctor's estate $300,000 for the lot. If you want to see the collection now, go to Tulsa, Oklahoma, and have a look at the Thomas Gilcrease Foundation.)

The doctor picked up a copy of the Russell book. "How much?" he asked.

When you get to be as old in sin as I, you have a feeling about buyers and their attraction for a given book. "Oh," I said, "I'll sell you one for a hundred dollars."

The doctor thought that over. "No, I won't pay that for one." Pause. I began mentally running over other people I could make the sale to.

"But I'll give you two hundred for both."

And the joke is that no other copy of the book has ever been found.

Marcus Whitman, the missionary, either did or did not save Oregon for the United States, depending on which school of historians you believe. However, neither school denies that he was the central figure in Oregon history.

At all events, the missionary societies of the time were so impressed with Brother Whitman that some of them asked a portrait painter named J. M. Stanley to go out to Walla Walla and paint the pioneer's portrait.

Just before Stanley got to Walla Walla, on November 30, 1847, a friendly Indian halted him and said that the Indians had just massacred Marcus Whitman and all his associates. Not unnaturally, Stanley told the news in a letter to a surviving fellow worker of Whitman's in Portland.

My last transaction with Fred Skiff consisted of a parcel containing Stanley's letter and some other material, with a note from Fred: "Charlie: I don't want any check; I want a money order for $250."

The Stanley letter is now in the William Robertson Coe collection in Yale University.

Unquestionably the world's finest collection of material relating to the American Indian, as well as the finest collections of Frederic Remington and Charlie Russell paintings and sculptures, is the Thomas Gilcrease Foundation in Tulsa, Oklahoma.

Thomas Gilcrease is an Oklahoma Indian. The majority of the Oklahoma Indian oil millionaires profited by the discovery of oil on the Indian reservations. Gilcrease, however, went down to Texas and found his own oil. He is extremely conscious of his Indian heritage, and his one interest in life is the assembling of material that will serve to inspire the Indians of the present day. The collections at the Gilcrease Foundation, therefore, portray the Indian from his own point of view, not as an anthropological curiosity.

I first heard of Thomas Gilcrease through an air-mail request for a copy of my catalogue. No one had ever asked me for a catalogue by air mail before, so I reciprocated by air mailing my catalogue of the Putnam collection of anthropology. This was the first time I had ever spent thirty cents to send out a catalogue.

Most such high-pressure sales efforts are wasted, but Mr. Gilcrease sent by return mail an order for several hundred dollars' worth of books. He kept on ordering from successive catalogues, and finally a bronzed stranger walked into the store and said, "I'm Gilcrease."

He had with him a list of books he wanted for his library. As he handed it to me, he said, "Mr. Everitt, I want you to remember that when you sell me a book, it must be not only a first edition but a fine copy."

I said, "Mr. Gilcrease, evidently you don't know very much about books."

"Just what do you mean by that?" he asked, bridling.

"Well, Jonathan Carver's *Travels* is one of the great books of western American history. The first edition is of no consequence at all. It's only when you get to the revised and enlarged third edition that you have a real cornerstone book. Or take Kendall's *Santa Fe Expedition*. You know the book, of course?"

"Yes, naturally."

"All right. The first edition is a fine book, but the seventh is worth ten times as much to anyone who looks past the price mark."

"I guess I shouldn't have said first edition. I should have said best edition," Mr. Gilcrease admitted with a smile.

One of the great Western paintings is Carl Wyman's *The Buffalo Hunt*. The picture has been famous for many years, and has been many times reproduced. Finally it turned up in the window of a 57th Street art gallery, marked five thousand dollars.

After some argument, I bought it for $800. I sent Mr. Gilcrease a photograph of it, and a quotation for $1250.

He happened to be in town a few days later, and handed me a check. As he was turning to leave, he said, "This may entertain you. I saw that painting in the gallery for five thousand, and was just about ready to buy it when the salesman got nervous and said, 'Possibly I can get this for you for three thousand.' I kind of lost interest then, not knowing what kind of place I might be in. Anyhow, I'm delighted to have the picture, and I hope you made a good commission."

Sometimes the only dependable rule I know about the *values* of Americana is that there is no rule of thumb. Perhaps the greatest delusion of all is that age has a bearing on value. Or that rarity has any relation to cash value.

A very large proportion of the earliest printing in America consisted of sermons and religious controversy, with an occasional schoolbook. Almost none of it has more than its scrap-paper value, and the few exceptions are valuable because the author, or perhaps the printer, was important, not because the text is worth reading.

I hope (though not very confidently) that you will not come to one of my fellow booksellers with a pamphlet "printed in Boston in the seventeen hundreds, with the *s*'s like *f*'s," and feel aggrieved at an actually generous offer of twenty-five cents.

As for rarity, single copies of most old newspapers are excessively rare, because people seldom take much care of last week's paper; they are also practically worthless in the rare-book trade, because they do not form a connected whole. Complete "runs" of newspapers are the prime examples of the rule that any collection is worth considerably more than the sum of its parts.

In this as in everything else about the rare-book business, the rules are like French irregular verbs — an inch of rule and a yard of exception.

I once paid a brother dealer a decent price for a John Adams letter, and he, perhaps partly relying on the rule about old newspapers, handed me a copy of the *Boston News-letter* for November 6, 1710, and said, "With my compliments." I did not throw it away because it had twelve pages instead of the ordinary four, and was entirely devoted to a British expedition against Canada. These oddities made me curious enough so that I wrote to the great authority on American newspapers for information.

He replied that he lacked this particular issue but that he made it a principle never to compete with a leading neighboring institution, which also lacked this issue. He suggested that his neighbor might be glad to pay as much as ten or fifteen dollars for the paper.

So I sat down and catalogued the *Boston News-letter* quite elaborately at eighty-five dollars.

The morning after the catalogue went out, Michael Walsh of Goodspeed's, Boston, telephoned to be first with his order. Once this formality was safely out of the way, he told me that the only other known copy was in the Public Record Office in London. It contained the first printing of Francis Nicholson's *Narrative of the Expedition against Port Royal,* which in itself is so rare as to be unrecorded.

Even the rule that you should collect Americana for the interest to be found in reading the books has many exceptions. I have had a lot of fun, and a lot of money, for example, out of imprints.

The "imprint" of a book is the information at the bottom of the title page — the publisher's name and the place and date of publication. In the book trade, imprints are books whose interest lies in the circumstances of their publication. Imprints are the basic and often the only foundation stones for the history of printing in America. The first publication in each state, territory, city, or even hamlet is interesting on its own account, and often very valuable as well.

The slow westward spread of printing in this country produced what seems like a fantastic disproportion in the values of imprints. Many New England imprints of 1750 are common as dirt, and not worth a quarter unless you want to hollow them out for a cigarette box. Southern imprints, which came somewhat later, were mostly laws and newspapers. Philadelphia imprints of 1800 are almost innumerable, yet those from Pittsburgh of that date are extreme rarities.

But the real rarities don't begin until you get past the Mississippi.

When I was helping in appraising William R. Coe's collection of Western Americana in preparation for his giving it to Yale, I came to a quarto broadside dated August 12, 1868.

I appraised it at fifteen hundred dollars, and thought afterward that perhaps I should have doubled or tripled the figure.

The sheet was titled: "Green River City Ordinances. Proclamation in Promulgation of the Laws and Ordinances passed by the Trustees of Green River City." The imprint reads: "Green River City, Dakota Territory." The broadside is one of two known items from the "press on wheels" of the Freeman brothers, who hauled their equipment in a wagon ahead of the Pacific Railroad construction gang. When the Freemans got to the railhead at Green River, the place was thus described by Hubert Howe Bancroft: "Shootings were frequent and every manner of vice abounded. The inhabitants were the scum of society and the accommodations for their shelter being tents and dugouts. A canvas saloon would answer as well as another for gambling, drinking and the practices of the dives. Nefarious men and women made the place intolerable. The city authorities were powerless, and robberies and assaults with deadly weapons were of daily and nightly occurrence. . . ."

The pillars of Green River society tried to clean up the place by issuing the laws found in the broadside.

The sprightlier elements wanted no laws of any kind, and they expressed their feelings by smashing the Freemans' press, thus making the Green River City Ordinances worth whatever price anyone wants to put on them. The Coe collection, incidentally, contains more unique imprints than any other collection in the world. I say this even though I am quite aware that the American Antiquarian Society at Worcester, Massachusetts, one of the great assemblages of Americana, was founded in 1813 by Isaiah Thomas, a great printer and the first historian of America's printing, with the gift of all his collection. The Antiquarian Society has been steadily, purposefully, and skillfully enlarging its collections for more than a century and a quarter. But it made the decision to collect no American imprints dated after 1820; consequently Mr. Coe, during part of his lifetime, was able to outrun the Society in the matter of unique imprints.

But remember, there are still no rules. West longitude alone does not account for all really rare imprints. One day in Chambersburg, Pennsylvania, I saw a store with a sign: ANY BOOK TEN CENTS, THREE FOR A QUARTER. Not wishing to be extravagant, I bought three.

One of these was an unexciting-looking pamphlet called *Miles' Overland Expedition to California,* printed in Chambersburg in 1851.

As I read the pamphlet on the train going home, I found

it an exciting original narrative; and then I began to wonder why it was not listed in any of the bibliographies of Western narratives. Then I remembered from my Civil War reading a book on the burning of Chambersburg. The place was entirely destroyed by the Confederates. I now think that Miles's pamphlet must have been stored in the back room of some printing shop, and practically all the copies must have gone up in smoke. Only two others have ever been found.

I sold my first copy to Henry R. Wagner (who described it for the first time in his famous bibliography, *The Plains and the Rockies*) for a thousand dollars.

I was still feeling quite pleased with myself for my discovery when I got a letter from Baltimore, offering me a long list of trash. Tucked away in the list, as casually as you please, was *Miles' Overland Expedition.*

I need hardly say that I was in Baltimore as fast as the first train would carry me. I went solemnly over all the books on the list, and then, pointing to the Miles book, remarked as casually as I could, "By the way, I don't see this thing here."

"Oh," said the owner, equally casually, "that's in the safe deposit vault." After some hours of high-level negotiation, during which I ceased to feel quite so smart, we settled on fifteen hundred dollars as a fair price.

Sometime on your travels, keep an eye out for a little imprint called *Three Years among the Indians,* by James, printed in Waterloo, Illinois, in 1846. I hope you will have as pleasant memories of your discovery as I have. A librarian friend in St. Louis let me know that the author's nephew was still living in Waterloo, that he had a copy of the pamphlet, which a scout had tried to buy from him, but he had said he could not bring himself to sell his uncle's book.

On the strength of this I went out to Waterloo, an inaccessible small town east of St. Louis. I was directed to a bungalow where an extremely nice old man asked what he could do for me.

"I've come to buy a book you don't want to sell," I said.

"We're just sitting down to corned beef and cabbage. Wouldn't you like some?" he asked. "How're you going to buy it? I'm just not going to sell it until I can get another copy."

"I don't know, but I'm not leaving without it."

"Well, how are you going to buy it?"

"I'm going to leave you a signed blank check," I said. "After you fill in the amount, and the check doesn't bounce from the bank, you mail me the pamphlet."

The old man looked at me with rather a twinkle. "What would you do," he asked, "if I filled that check in for three hundred dollars?"

"Try it, and you'll see," said I. I handed him the blank check, thanked him for the corned beef, and went back to St. Louis. Five or six weeks later the check had still not cleared, and I began to worry about *Three Years among the Indians.*

At last a letter came from the nephew, in which he said he had decided to open a bank account with the amount of my check, but had not cared to do it in a small town where everyone knew everyone else's business. So he had opened a new account in St. Louis, my check had cleared, and he was sending me *Three Years among the Indians* by express, insured, collect.

Another thing that lends spice to the pursuits of the imprint collector is the fact that one imprint may be dear at five dollars, and the same title, printed the same year but in a different place, may be worth five hundred. There is an Indian treaty printed in London in 1756 that you can find almost at will for about fifty dollars. It is almost impossible to set any price on the identical treaty, printed the same year in Williamsburg, Virginia, because only two copies are known. The first one appeared in the famous Brinley sale in 1881, and the second passed over my desk at a great bargain for some hundreds of dollars a few years ago.

As you will learn if you read to the end of this book, I have very little patience with people who say that all the killings and all the discoveries have been made. But I must admit that the collecting of imprints has grown up like a mushroom in the last twenty-five years; you could hardly do now what my partner Adolph Stager and I did at the old Stan V. Henkels auction rooms about 1925. A bundle of forty-five pamphlets, worth from five to fifty dollars each, was up for sale. Stager nervously telephoned me just before the sale to find out how much money we had in the bank, in case we should have to reach for this prize.

Right after the sale he telephoned again, almost equally nervous with relief: he had bought the lot for forty-five dollars.

We thought it was a pretty good haul until the morning after, when we really began scrutinizing our loot. Then we found that it included a copy of the first Mormon Constitution, printed in Kanesville in 1849. This, like the Green River Ordinances, was printed on a migratory press, and not only the press but the town had long since ceased to exist.

After some digging around, I priced the pamphlet at a thousand dollars. George W. Cole, the librarian of the Huntington Library, San Marino, California, thought the price was ridiculous; but when I put the pamphlet in the American Art Association's auction soon afterward, Mr. Huntington's agent bought it—for $1010. Counting the buying agent's commission, it cost him $111 not to buy the pamphlet from me in the first place.

United States government documents are probably the most forbidding-looking lot of publications you will find anywhere. Most of them are badly printed, festooned with certificates, letters of transmittal, and mysterious code numbers. Probably more than 50 per cent are also pure hot air – speeches by members of Congress happy to get their names in print for the one time in their lives.

The funny thing is that literally nobody knows what gold is buried in those hills of paper. The most vital sources for our history are to be found nowhere else.

You might naturally think that a person could go to the Library of Congress and say, "Here, fetch me the Government documents on so and so."

But you would be wrong. There is no complete record of what documents were published. A versatile old character named Ben Perley Poore put out a bibliography in the eighties, covering perhaps 75 per cent of the items now known. There have been some later bibliographies, but none even so full as Poore's.

Here are a few documents that pop into my head as I sit here.

The first American treason trial, that of William Blount, of Tennessee, in the 1790's, is known to us only through a Government publication.

The Government published the first record of the Lewis and Clark expedition.

The only existing records of the Old Northwest are in dusty government folios.

All we knew about Japan for fifty years was contained in the three fat volumes of Commodore Matthew Calbraith Perry's report on his expedition that opened up Nippon to the west. (Among the numerous plates in the first edition was a picture showing Japanese men and women bathing together in a steam bath. This was the only thing the Japanese government objected to, and it was omitted from later printings.)

So far as I can see, the subject of Government documents will always remain a Chinese puzzle, yielding a nugget here and there to those persistent enough to dig for it.

My interest was first aroused thirty or forty years ago, when several hundred folio documents were bundled and offered for sale at the American Art Association. William L. Clements, of Ann Arbor, Michigan, sent me a substantial bid, remarking at the same time that he wanted to complete his files of Government documents printed before 1800. I bought in the lot for a mere fraction of his bid. Before I shipped his purchase, I looked through the collection and decided that it was practically hopeless for me ever to learn anything about American history. Even now I don't know whether the Clements collection is finished up to 1800. For that matter, I wonder if the Library of Congress has a complete file.

Recently I have had a phone call from the Southern Book Company in Baltimore, asking me to guess at the value of a Government document on the Bill of Rights, of which the only other known copy is in the Library of Congress.

All I could say was, "I'm damned if I know. It's all a question of how far your imagination works, with a minimum of five thousand dollars."

One of the great sources for the history of the Northwest is the report of the expedition under Commodore Wilkes. It was first printed in five volumes, plus an atlas, then reprinted several times in five volumes with the maps bound in. Ed

Eberstadt found out somehow that there had been an edition of a hundred sets printed the year before the well-known edition. There were also innumerable volumes of scientific reports in folio from the various experts who accompanied the expedition. These too were printed in an edition of one hundred.

I have never seen the edition that Eberstadt discovered; but I have, I am sorry to say, seen two sets of the scientific reports.

The first set was in the duplicate room at Cornell University. The librarian, Mr. Harris, asked me, "Shall I put these along with the wastepaper?"

Here was one of the insoluble dilemmas in a bookseller's work. If I offered ten dollars, I would unquestionably get them – and be remembered forevermore as a robber of widows and orphans and librarians. Whatever I said was wrong.

So I made the other mistake. I said, "I hardly think I would do that. I can give you five hundred for the set."

Mr. Harris said, "I'll have to let you know." As soon as I had waked him up, he remembered that the books were not duplicates but simply bulky, dreary-looking tomes that he had got tired of giving shelf space to.

The only other set I ever saw was in the basement of the Rhode Island Historical Society. I had practically the same experience, was equally sure I could get away with them for ten dollars, and offered five hundred. Later, hoping against hope to get some action out of the librarian, I wrote and offered a thousand. This was some ten years ago, and so far I am still waiting for an answer.

To my great regret I am forced to confess that my own book is a sad example in one respect; if I had kept a diary during my sixty years, instead of just trying to remember back now, the story would really have meant something. Old men's recollections are plentiful enough among historical books, but the real nuggets are the things that were scrawled down at the time. From a historical standpoint you can easily see why this is, and I have had experiences enough to show that it is also true in respect to money values.

Fred Skiff showed me a tiny notebook, not altogether unlike those you buy in dime stores now. The inside was scribbled in pencil. Every attic has a dozen of them, usually containing notes on the weather and the price of eggs.

"Charlie, get me twenty-five hundred for this," said Fred.

"Why?"

"Look on page fifty-nine."

Page fifty-nine showed that the diarist had got lost in the California mountains in January, 1848. To his considerable relief he was rescued by some Indians working for a man named Sutter and brought into Sutter's Fort on the twenty-second, two days before the man came in with the first gold nuggets. About three lines of the diary were devoted to the excitement when one of Sutter's employees, named Marshall, came back into camp with some gold nuggets he had found. I had the diary on my desk when Dr. Rosenbach's assistant came prospecting around, as he frequently did. He looked at the book.

"How much?"

"Oh, I don't know."

The usual procedure was scrupulously followed: he went home, and Dr. Rosenbach telephoned to ask if I would come and show him the diary. He sent his Rolls-Royce.

We talked for a while about nothing in particular.

"How much for this?" the doctor finally asked.

"Three thousand five hundred."

"If you'll give me 10 per cent off, I'll write you a check."

"Oh, go peddle your newspapers, Doc." I went out and down the marble stairs.

"I suppose you think I'm being foolish not to buy this," said Dr. Rosenbach, patting me condescendingly on the shoulder.

"No, I don't think you're being foolish. I know you're being foolish. It's just a question of whether I sell it to Henry E. Huntington for five thousand or you sell it to him for ten thousand."

He laughed, and swung me around to face upstairs again. I suppose my price must have been ten times the value of any nugget found the first day of the Gold Rush.

A Midwestern librarian friend of mine was looking busily for a copy of Larned's *Literature of American History* (one of the most useful books any bookseller can own, incidentally), and could not find one.

I had just been an underbidder for a Connecticut library in which was a copy of the Larned, so I suggested that the librarian write to the successful buyer, a woman in Hartford. He did so, and she surprised me very much by selling him the book for two dollars. This pleased me only moderately because I would have been glad to give her twenty dollars, but, anyway, my friend had his Larned.

Shortly afterwards he sent me a book with a note: "Please take this with my compliments; I found it out here on a ten-cent shelf." The book looked quite unpromising. It was *Recollections of a Woman of Eighty-five,* by Mrs. Nye-Starr, Chicago, 1881. When I looked at it, I discovered that along with the recollections of an octogenarian was a diary she had kept as a young girl on her way out to join her brother, who was governor of Nevada. She had met Mark Twain in his Western days, and her diary told all about it. The book wound up in the Coe collection at Yale. Perhaps because a Chicago book of

1881 looks so commonplace that you would pass it by on a ten-cent counter, no other copy has ever been unearthed, though I have advertised twenty times and canvassed all my librarian friends around Chicago.

Some high-powered papers are really too hot to handle. At the time of the Hay-Pauncefote Treaty in 1901, we had an ambassador in London by the name of White, who came from Englewood, New Jersey.

Years afterward, Sam Dauber went on a fishing trip to the Salvation Army in Englewood and returned with a letter book containing copies of all the secret correspondence regarding the Hay-Pauncefote Treaty. After looking through the papers, you could not escape the conclusion that this treaty was one of the great scandals in American history.

Sam was feeling pretty pleased with himself. "We ought to make some money out of this," he said.

"Sam, you've got an elephant by the tail, and you can't let go. If you catalogue it, the Government will claim it, sure. What else can you do with it?"

At length someone from an Eastern university came into the store, and I showed him our firecracker. "What would you do with this?"

He did not know, any more than I did. Finally he and Sam Dauber and I sat down and after arguing for an hour, I said, "Well, we'll sell this to the university if they'll promise not to let anyone see it for twenty years."

That was the deal; the twenty years are not up yet.

A president of the Theosophical Society, Claude Wright, disappeared, leaving two trunks behind him. They were finally auctioned off by a University Place gallery for storage charges.

Sam Dauber, a good gambler, bought them in for thirty dollars.

When we broke the trunks open, about all we found was something that had been a dress suit before the moths moved in.

Sam is also a great hand for the follow-up. He went over to the auctioneer's, choosing a moment when the great man was absent, and asked one of the boys around the place if there had not been any papers in the trunks.

"Oh, yes," said the boy. "We put these over in a corner."

"Thank you very much," said Sam, peeling off two dollars for future protection.

When we started rooting through the papers, we found that they recorded many of the vitriolic quarrels among Annie Besant and Madame Blavatsky's other followers. "I am the true successor to Madame Blavatsky," wrote Annie Besant. "You are, like hell," replied somebody else. "I have her ring, which I took off her finger when she was lying in her coffin." And so on and so on.

"Well," I told Sam, "we've got thirty-two dollars in this; let's see if we can get fifteen hundred out of it."

I was just preparing to catalogue the lot when a six-foot stranger came in the store and downstairs to the rare-book department.

"I hear you have some theosophical papers," he said. "How much do you want for them?"

"Well, I was just getting ready to catalogue them," I said; "but to save the trouble and expense, I'll let you have the lot for a thousand dollars."

"What? Trying to blackmail me?" shouted the stranger.

"Do you see those steps?" I shouted back. "You get up them in a hurry, you son of a bitch, or I'll throw you up."

An hour or two later he was back, perfectly placid. "I've been asking around to see what kind of fellow you are. I'll give you a thousand dollars for the papers, if you'll tear them up in my presence."

"I'm letting you off fairly easy," I said, "because before you came in, I had just about decided to ask fifteen hundred. But you'll still save my cataloguing the papers. It's a deal."

I carefully blotted his check, and then set to work tearing the theosophical papers into small snippets.

On the corner of Charing Cross Road and Shaftesbury Avenue is a famous pub. When I was in London about 1925, a number of my dealer friends and I used to go there regularly after the shops closed at seven.

One night I noticed a young man in the corner who looked as if he lacked the price of a drink. In Yankee fashion and British phrase I said, "Won't you join us in a spot?"

The young man said he would be delighted, and introduced himself, saying his name was Falconer.

English drinking parties run to about one drink per hour. He had put away one spot when we all decided our time was up. He thanked me again, and started to leave.

Something put it into my head to ask, "By the way, are you any connection of Judge Falconer, the one that traveled around New Mexico with a tin bathtub, and kept falling off his horse?"

"As a matter of fact, I'm the last living descendant of Judge Falconer, and I even have his papers."

Trying not to look as excited as I felt, I said in what I hoped was a steady voice, "How about a spot of lunch at the Horseshoe tomorrow?"

"Gladly," he said, and so we parted.

One of the great books of Western travel, which was reprinted several times in its own day and has lost none of its value since, is George W. Kendall's *Narrative of the Texan-Santa Fe Expedition.* In it he refers several times to the eccentric Englishman, Falconer, with the tin bathtub. As a steady reader of Kendall, I remembered Falconer; hence my question to the young man.

Back at the hotel that night, I tried to calm myself. "Look," I said to my wife, but really to myself, "you don't just stumble onto things like this. This is too easy; there's something wrong with it."

In the morning I rushed over to see Leon Kashnor at the Museum Book Store. "Do you know a young fellow named Falconer, Leon?" I asked.

"Oh, for Christ's sake, Charlie, you stay clear of that," Leon said. "I've fifty pounds in the man now, and I haven't the slightest idea whether he owns a single sheet of paper."

I went to lunch at the Horseshoe, carefully chatted about everything in the world except the Falconer papers, quietly dodged an attempt by the lineal descendant to put the bite on me, and went about my business. I had finally convinced myself that it really was too good to be true, so I could keep my disappointment within bounds.

Three years later Leon Kashnor welcomed me at the door of his shop with a small handful of papers. "Well, here are the Falconer papers. They stood me eighty quid, and I certainly hope you can think of some way to get me out whole."

When I went through the bundle, I found two items that looked valuable from a money standpoint. One was a two-page letter from Falconer telling about the Santa Fe expedition. The other, also in Falconer's own hand, was a bibliography of his writings. (After he got back from America, he became a judge, and wrote a great many legal pamphlets.) The rest of the papers showed that Falconer had been a British secret agent on the Mexican border at the time he was with the Santa Fe expedition.

The bibliographer remarked that Falconer's own account of his New Mexico trip had been printed in New Orleans. This Leon and I already knew, because the Falconer pamphlet is among the rarest of books. But then he went on to say that the same material had been added also to the seventh edition of Kendall. Since no bookseller ever glances inside late editions of a book, this was complete news to us. The seventh edition of Kendall, of course, was very much looked down on by all the people who wanted a first edition, and the price of the seventh stood at about five dollars.

A lawyer friend of mine, Lanman Crosby, has always amused himself by spending his spare time in bookshops. I told him about the seventh edition of Kendall, and between us we dug up seven sets in the next three years, which we were able to sell at fifty dollars a set instead of five. We must have done a thorough job, because I haven't seen a seventh edition of Kendall in the last five years.

The letter that was the other prominent item among the Falconer papers I sold for five hundred dollars to a Texas collector. Leon and I both came out more than whole from the transaction.

While the collection was intact in my hands, I called up Dr. Frederick Hodge and asked if he would like to edit the Falconer letters. He said he had been meaning to do it for years. So Dauber & Pine issued *The Falconer Letters and Notes* in an edition of 250 copies, printed in 1930. This little book is now quite as rare as the seventh edition of Kendall's expedition.

* * *

One of the most famous professional book-hunters of the period around 1910, who worked a great deal for me, happened to be traveling through Connecticut, where he encountered a Civil War collector named Eldridge. Eldridge's collection was unrivaled in its time, but it simply could not be bought. The book-hunter, while unsuccessful in buying the collection, made the acquaintance of Miss Eldridge and later married her.

Among the gems of the collection was a set of Civil War photographs by Matthew Brady, easily five times larger than that of any contemporary. After Eldridge died, his son-in-law, as executor, took the Brady photographs to Lanier of the *Review of Review* and sold them to him for thirty thousand dollars. Lanier rounded up some lesser collections, and poured them all into the *Photographic History of the Civil War.*

He made a splendid job of it, and sold so many thousands of sets that for ten years afterwards a bookseller seldom bought a private library that did not contain at least one set of the *Photographic History of the Civil War.*

Naturally this drove the price down; I have seen many sets sell for $3.50.

It was a really good book, and times have changed. Sometime when you have nothing else to do, go hunting for a *Photographic History* under $50 a set.

In the process of preparing the *Photographic History* for publication, the editors tossed out some three thousand photographs as not being originals — that is, they were photographs of photographs. This lot was put up at auction and sold for a small sum.

The great backer of the Western Reserve Historical Society in those days was president of the American Steel and Wire Company, William P. Palmer. His main interest was enlarging a collection at the Historical Society which covered both sides of the Civil War. At the time, I knew he had spent about $30,000 on it.

I happened to be in Cleveland, so I went to call on my chum Wallace Cathcart, the librarian of the Society. He said, "Come on upstairs. Mr. Palmer wants you to see his Civil War stuff."

I looked over the material, and Mr. Palmer asked what I thought of it.

"Well," I said, "I think you've made a fine beginning." He grinned a little at that. "Now," he said, "I want to show you a collection of Brady photographs that I bought at a bargain recently for several thousand dollars."

Sure enough, it was our old friends.

Mr. Palmer showed me a letter from a book man whom we'll call John Doe: "This is unquestionably the finest lot of Brady photographs ever offered for sale, and I am prepared to guarantee that each and every one is an original."

To my friend Cathcart's chagrin, I said, "I'm willing to give you a different guarantee. I will personally guarantee that you do not have a single original Brady photograph in the entire lot."

Mr. Palmer just grinned, and said, "We do get trimmed a lot, don't we?"

Not all Clevelanders were so good-natured about it. I was in Cathcart's office when an elderly lawyer came in with a list of books he wanted to sell. "Doe offered me twelve hundred and fifty," he said.

"Here, Charlie, you take a look at the list," Cathcart put in.

"Oh, I don't need to do that. If John Doe will pay twelve hundred fifty, I'll give two thousand without bothering to look at the list," I said.

"No," the lawyer said, "I won't take that offer. What I will do is to sell you the lot for twelve hundred fifty, and I will pack and ship them at my expense, just so that son of a bitch doesn't get them in Cleveland."

My last transaction with John Doe, the dealer, was a fairly complete joke on me. While I was at Dauber & Pine's, I catalogued an extraordinary copy of Doddridge's *Indian Wars* at seventy-five dollars. I showed it to Sam Dauber and said, "Take a look at this, because you'll never see another copy as good."

John Doe wired for it.

Three months later a copy came back, with no covers, library discard stamps smeared all over it, and a note from him, saying, "Charlie, what do you mean by cataloguing this as the finest copy you ever saw?"

For want of any other excitement, I decided I would sue him. A Western lawyer happened to be in the store, and I said, "I'll give you half of the sixty-seven fifty if you'll collect this." I reached into my pocket and found three ten-dollar bills.

"Oh, that's plenty," said the lawyer. "I'll collect it."

That is the last I have heard of Doddridge or lawyer.

One of the first things I discovered when I began to read American history seriously in 1891 was that everything in my school history books was at least questionable. It took me twenty years to unlearn everything that had been stuffed down my throat.

Perhaps my hypersensitivity to some of our well-advertised historical monuments is a drawback that goes with dealing in the stuff of American history, but it also has its compensations. My Labrador retriever, like anyone else, enjoys a comfort stop now and then on a long drive. I have always found great pleasure as we pass through Tarrytown, New York, in accommodating him by a stop at the monument to the captors of Major André.

The facts of the famous capture are well known, though perhaps not in all their details. The three great patriots who captured André really did capture him, but they were sutlers and, not to put too fine a point on it, bootleggers. André offered them a large bribe to let him go, and their first instinct was to escort him safely to the British lines. Halfway there, however, they began to think they would not look very good if they were captured; so they decided to go down in history as heroes by taking him to the American army.

It is barely possible that the members of the D.A.R. and the S.A.R. will not approve of this last paragraph; but then, I am not looking for them to read this book, anyway.

The bulk of the legends printed in our schoolbooks are about as accurate as Emanuel Leutze's famous painting of *Washington Crossing the Delaware.* Some years ago one of our best sellers was a book called *1776;* the thing I remember best about it is the author's statement, concerning the painting, that in the first place Washington knew far too much to stand up in a rowboat and that in the second place he would probably have been facing the rear, shouting at the 250-pound General Henry Knox, "Move your fat ass, and trim the boat."

The late Mr. Frank Reynolds, who was a partner in the travel firm called Ask Mr. Foster, made a hobby of Florida history. Probably no one has ever known more about the subject. He wrote the standard history of St. Augustine, and in the course of his research spent some years on the "Oldest House in America." Perhaps as a relaxation from his larger history, he wrote and published a pamphlet characterizing the Oldest House as undoubtedly a fake. He used to give the pamphlet away by the hundreds at his various offices, and he would send me four or five hundred at a crack for free distribution.

A St. Augustine tourist organization threatened to sue him; he told them he wished they would. The only thing that ever happened was a letter from Chauncey M. Depew, the New York Central Railroad magnate, who was also an active figure in the Florida Historical Society. "Why destroy pleasant legends?" said the old robber baron.

What makes me mad is that the writers of the history books on which our children are brought up seem to prefer Chauncey Depew's attitude to Mr. Reynolds's and mine. Not only the capture of Major André and the Oldest House but the heart-stirring stories of Betsy Ross and Barbara Frietchie are practically pure products of folk imagination. If any reader of mine can produce the slightest evidence that Betsy Ross ever saw an American flag, I will willingly send him a genuine *Bay Psalm Book,* with a presentation autograph by Stephen Daye, who printed it.

For a good deal less than that, I will find you part of the Book of Mormon that was printed some months before John Smith received the communication from on high.

All the orthodox accounts tell us that the golden plates on which the Book of Mormon was inscribed were found in a hill near Palmyra, New York, in the spring of 1830. (They were written in a foreign tongue, but the angel obligingly provided Smith with a magic crystal through which he could read and transcribe them in English.)

I have never investigated the matter of the discovery, but I did once chance upon a magazine called *The Reflector* that began publication at Palmyra in 1829. The November, 1829, issue contained an early section of the Book of Mormon –

which, incidentally, the newspapers of the time regarded and criticized as a political pamphlet.

Perhaps the pleasantest thing about *The Reflector* is that it reminds me of my many years' friendship with Herbert Auerbach, the greatest collector of Mormon books who has ever lived. The connection is a trifle roundabout.

My friend and factotum, Harry Alpern, once spent an extremely discouraging week in his long round of attics, antique and junk shops. All he had to show for six days of unremitting labor was one forlorn volume of *The Reflector*. As a matter of course, I offered it first to Mr. Auerbach, who thanked me, but said he had a copy.

(He told me later how he had come by his. A penciled post card arrived in the mail from Palmyra, listing some old books that an elderly lady wanted to sell. Mr. Auerbach did not write, he did not wire, he did not telephone; he went in person to make sure of that haul. The old lady was very much astonished when Mr. Auerbach gave her fifty dollars for a dog-eared old magazine.)

My next move was to write a careful description of the book for Mr. Littel, of Chicago, with a $175 tag. He bought it.

When later his books were sent to the Parke-Bernet Galleries, the auctioneer picked out all the better items to be catalogued and sold separately. The odds and ends were being bundled when a cataloguer happened to find my description stuck into the volume of *The Reflector*. He thereupon catalogued it very elaborately by itself, and the Scribner Book Store bid it in for $450.

The Auerbach copy was sold later for $400. In the same sale was a run of a weekly newspaper called *The Valley Tan*, named after a cheap brand of whisky made in Utah. Some eccentric launched the paper to attack the Mormons. He kept going for a full year, fifty-two numbers, and Mr. Auerbach had forty-nine. I ought to know; I sold them to him.

One day, in response to a note, I called at a broken-down Southern mansion near Charlottesville, Virginia. The lady of the house welcomed me at the door. "Before I come in," I said, "I want to tell you that I'm fed up with you Southern ladies."

"What's the matter with us, Mr. Everitt?"

"It doesn't matter what book I try to buy below the Mason and Dixon's line, it always belonged to Grandpappy and isn't for sale."

"You won't have that trouble here," she said. "You can buy anything in the house."

I went into a large library, which was almost entirely filled with junk. The only exceptions were the lady's husband, who was sitting in the corner, and three volumes of Ben Franklin's newspapers, sitting on the floor. She said, "Mr. Everitt, what are you going to give me for those?"

"One hundred fifty for these," I said.

"Oh, is that all?"

I turned to her husband. "Listen to the woman," I said. "She knew I was going to offer her three dollars, so when I offer her a hundred and fifty, which is halfway honest, she say's 'Is that all?' "

"Mr. Everitt," he said, "you could have bought those for two dollars."

"Now," I said, "I am going out in the woodshed."

"You can't do that," she told me. "It's getting dark."

I repeated that I was going into the woodshed to see what she had thrown away. After some argument she got me a lantern.

"Don't worry," I said. "I've been in a lot dirtier places than your woodshed looking for books."

In a wood-basket, ready to start the next morning's fire, was this file of *The Valley Tan,* the only approximately complete one yet traced.

I went back into the house. "Now," I told the lady, "I'm going to rob you. If these had been in the library, I'd have given you fifty dollars for them. Because you were going to burn them up in the morning, I'm going to give you ten."

"Don't you think you're being pretty cruel?"

"I think it serves you right," her husband put in.

A letter came in one day from a perfect stranger in Brunswick, Maine, with a list of books he wanted to sell. He had a three-volume Bishop's *American Manufactures* (worth $30 or $40), for $3.00; Hodge's *Handbook of American Indians* (a $15 book), for $1.50; and twenty or thirty other books of about the same grade, similarly priced.

I wrote back and said I hoped he had not sent out other copies of his list, but in any case I would be happy to pay him $15 for the Bishop; $7.50 for the Hodge; and so on through the list. My offer was about double his total.

He answered that this was the only list he had sent out, that he felt a bit uneasy about it, and that he would gladly accept my offer, or his own original prices. So I sent him the full amount of my offer.

Not long afterward he telephoned me from the Plaza Hotel in New York. After telling me that I had paid for his visit, he went on to say that he had some old letters he wished I would look over. When I got there, he had a sort of sea chest full of thousands of letters and manuscripts from the first American missionary to Persia. There were manuscripts of the first translation of the Bible into Persian, and heaven knows what else.

"I paid a dollar for these," he said. "Do you want to give me a hundred?"

I said, "Fine, how do we get them to the store?"

"I'll take care of that."

He hoisted the sea chest on his shoulder, tipped someone a dime to help him into a cab with it, and off we went.

Going over in the taxi, he said, "There's one stamp in this envelope that I think is pretty good." The stamp was a New York Provisional of 1845. Later one of the largest stamp dealers in town dropped in, looked the stamp over, and exclaimed plaintively that it had been folded. The most he could pay for it was thirty dollars.

A friend of mine who does not share my detestation for stamps took this one down to Nassau Street, went to fourteen dealers, and emerged triumphant with $57.50.

The box of missionary letters I catalogued at $450. The Library of Congress asked to see them on approval. This was before my little private lobby had finagled through a law prohibiting them from keeping approval items more than seven days, and their habit was to hang on to things from six months to two years. So I said no thank you to the Library of Congress.

Some weeks later the librarian of a theological seminary in New England telephoned, asking if she might have the letters on approval for sixty days, until the Oriental scholars on the faculty came back from vacation.

Some two months later she phoned again to say that their scholars all agreed on the great value of the material, but with all their efforts they had not succeeded in raising more than four hundred dollars.

"I think it is so important for the right institution to have these letters," I told her, "that I should like to contribute a hundred dollars to your fund myself. The letters are yours for three hundred."

My friend from Brunswick had other treasures of the same sort in store for me. I went to see him at his bungalow in Brunswick. He showed me a bureau drawer full of letters from the golden age of New England—Alcott, forty letters from one of F.D.R.'s Delano ancestors, describing his adventures in California, and enough more to fill the drawer.

"Everitt, I won't sell you these," he said.

I had just discovered that he was a teetotaler, so I was undoubtedly in disgrace. I tried to put a good face on it. "All right. I've never committed suicide yet because I couldn't buy anything. So what did you get me here for?"

He poured us each a Coca-Cola. "I won't sell them to you. What I want is that you take them and give me half of anything you get."

(I forget whether it was two or three thousand dollars that we finally split.)

Then he told me he had a barnful of books down in the village. My train was due to leave in two hours.

Pushing to the utmost my eagle eye for shelf-backs, I snatched a hundred odd volumes off his shelves. One of these was a small morocco folio in Sheraton style, with lettering on the front cover: "The Secretary of State."

"Would you like me to give you a hundred dollars for this lot?" I asked.

"Hell," he said, "you can have the whole barnful for that."

But I stuck to my offer and made up an express package out of my choice. "Who pays for the express?" asked my friend.

I said I would. When the package reached me in New York, I grabbed hastily for the small folio. I had carefully refrained from looking inside it in Brunswick, but I was sure I had recognized it as *Laws of a Congress of the U.S.*, New York, 1789. There is nothing very rare about the title, but a binding especially lettered for the Secretary of State is another matter. The Secretary then was Thomas Jefferson.

Before I glanced at the cover, I had decided that this was one of the most valuable books ever to pass through my hands. Here was my year's overhead in one neat package.

Then I looked inside. Some Yankee from the state of Maine had torn out every second page, and had pasted on all the others such items of prose and verse as seemed to his peanut brain worth preserving.

As I was inspecting this glorious scrapbook, a dealer looked over my shoulder. "I'll give you a hundred dollars for it, as is," he said.

I was so disgusted that I instantly wrapped the book up and sent it, with my compliments, to my old friend Dr. Randolph G. Adams, of the William L. Clements Library at Ann Arbor, Michigan.

Later he sent me a careful description of the book. The gist of it was as follows:

> Not only was it bound specially for the Secretary of State, but that Secretary, Thomas Jefferson, actually used this copy, as is evidenced from a brief marginal manuscript note on p. 15 which is unmistakably in Jefferson's hand. This came to light upon the removal of some awful poem.
>
> BIBLIOGRAPHICALLY SPEAKING: This book was originally issued in marbled paper covers. But apparently copies were especially bound for Federal officials – as this one for "The Secretary of State." There should be 53 leaves, of which our criminal has removed 26.

There probably were other copies in this rather fine early American binding, Sheraton style, for other Federal officials. George Washington's copy, which Griffin & Lane in their description of Washington's Library said was missing in 1897 when they made their checklist. It was appraised at $.75 at the time of the settlement of Washington's will.

This book disproves Dr. Rosenbach's story as to his book (mentioned in the *Book-Hunter's Holiday*) being the only book which survived the fire of 1814. This one obviously did also. Perhaps I should use an early nineteenth-century hand, and write in it "Picked up by me during the conflagration incident to the burning of Washington, 1814, C.P.E."

Morton Pennypacker, the great Long Island collector, came into Dauber & Pine's one day with an abridged juvenile edition of *Robinson Crusoe*, printed in New York by Hugh Gaine, the celebrated Tory printer, in 1774.

"Half the frontispiece to this is gone," said Pennypacker, "so I'd be happy to take ten dollars for it."

Considering how many editions of *Robinson Crusoe* there are, you might have hesitated to pay ten cents; but I happened to know that this was one of the possibly two or three Hugh Gaine imprints that the New York Public Library lacked. I called in my friend R. W. G. Vail, who worked there at the time, and asked him to offer it to Mr. Eames at sixty dollars. Mr. Vail later wrote me a letter about the transaction.

Mr. Eames was quite excited about it, never having heard of a copy of this, the first American edition of *Robinson Crusoe*. He said that the price was very modest, so sent me on to Dr. V. H. Paltsits, head of the American History and Rare Book division. Dr. Paltsits willingly approved the purchase and sent me on to H. M.

Lydenberg, then head of the Reference Department, for final approval. I had just convinced Mr. Lydenberg that we should buy the book, since we had a fine collection of Gaine imprints and also of early American juveniles, when the Director, Mr. E. H. Anderson, happened in and wanted to know what the book was we were discussing. I explained the case to him, and he, not being a book man and having little interest in rare books as such, said: "We cannot spend our money for a little, abbreviated, child's edition. We have many other complete editions including the first English edition." I tried to convince him that we should purchase it, and explained that it was the only known copy, but he refused to let us buy it. I then said that, if the library would not buy it, I would purchase it myself as a speculation. He said if I could make anything after paying such a high price for it, I was welcome to do so. Soon after, a woman free-lance newspaper writer came to the library looking for material, and I showed her the *Robinson Crusoe.* She got excited about it and wrote a good feature article about it in which she said it might bring as much as $10,000. A few days later Dr. Rosenbach saw me at an auction and said: "I hear you picked up an early *Robinson Crusoe.* What are you going to do with it—you don't collect juveniles." I said that I had not decided what to do with it and he suggested that I bring it up and show it to him, which I agreed to do. A couple of weeks later I went up to his office and spent a delightful couple of hours haggling over it. I offered it at $1200, and he began very low, probably around $50 or $100, I don't remember the amount. The upshot of it all was that I sold it to him for $600, then took his check down and showed it to Mr. Anderson at the library, to his great astonishment.

Some time later, I went to London, and was welcomed by my old friend Ben Marks with a newspaper clipping that read: "AMERICAN BOOKSELLER SELLS $5000 BOOK FOR $50."

"Hell, Ben, think nothing of it," I said. "I do that every day."

The old rule held good again here: no sooner had Rosenbach bought his copy than Yale bought a perfect copy.

Anyone who lives in Manhattan naturally dreads like the plague having to go to Brooklyn. Nevertheless, during the fifteen or twenty years that the bookshop of Neil Morrow Ladd on upper Fulton Street was in existence, any dealer or collector who did not fight his way to Brooklyn at least once a week was very foolish. Fred Ladd had two men on the road all the time, and several hundred new volumes always came in every week. He had a corner where he used to stack any Americana he was doubtful about until I could take a look at them.

On one of my last trips to his shop, I had inspected what he had, and was ready to leave, when he said, "You'd better take a look at this, hadn't you?"

He pointed to a set of Shakespeare.

In my opinion, sets of Shakespeare are usually too thin even to make good doorstops unless you pile several volumes together; but since Ladd asked me, I looked. Inside the front cover of Volume I was an inscription to James Russell Lowell from his loving parents on the occasion of his entering Harvard College. Scattered through all the volumes were some twelve hundred notes in Lowell's hand. Here, obviously, was the source from which he had drawn much of the material for his *English Dramatists.*

I quaked to think what Fred would want for the set. "How much, Fred?" I asked.

"Well, I think if I put this set up at auction, it would probably bring me at least seventy-five dollars."

"You mean you'll take seventy-five dollars for it now, or what?"

"Why, yes," said Fred. "I'd be glad to take seventy-five dollars for it."

Naturally one of my first acts after closing the sale was to write to Amy Lowell. She came down from Cambridge especially to see the set.

At the store she lit up one of her black cigars.

She sat there puffing, and finally came to the inevitable question: "How much?"

"Twelve hundred and fifty," I suggested.

She barely interrupted her puffing enough to say, "Why, hell's bells, you're the goddamnedest thief and robber I ever heard of. But I'll take it."

Frank Dobie once very truly remarked that luck consists in being ready for the chance. He also remarked that 90 per cent of all the great discoveries are made by pure accident.

Among my closest bookseller friends is John Scopes, of Albany, one of the dozen greatest living Americana dealers in the world. On one occasion I spent several hours with him and turned up a number of very nice rarities. As I was catching my breath, I glanced idly at a ten-cent counter near the door, which I know is always a waste of time. For some reason or other I picked up a little 16mo entitled *Life of Louis Tarascon.* It said nothing to me, but I riffled the pages with one motion, as I always do, and the word "Oregon" jumped out at me.

I solemnly handed John Scopes a dime. "Oh, the hell with that," said he.

"No," I said, "the price is a dime, and a dime it is."

On the train coming down the Hudson I was finally reduced to reading my ten-cent book. It developed that Louis Tarascon was a man who lived in Louisville before the Civil War, and he had a land scheme for colonizing Oregon.

On my next visit from Henry R. Wagner, the great bibliographer of the West, I had brother Tarascon lying on my desk.

His eyes lit up with no attempt at concealment, and he actually seemed rather relieved when I consented to sell him the book for $250.

As I was pocketing his check and he was pocketing his book, he remarked condescendingly, "Of course you'll never see it, but Tarascon put some of this stuff into a broadside that was printed at Louisville the year before the book was."

Gratuitous insults like that, particularly when linked with bits of information, have a way of sinking into my mind. Possibly six months later I was canvassing my friend Liebschutz's bookstore in Louisville. He had a bound volume of pamphlets that excited him very much because it contained three presentation sermons from Ralph Waldo Emerson.

To me, these were just good standard merchandise, but I gave the volume my customary riffle, and caught a flash of a broadside signed by Louis Tarascon. For the sake of appearances I chaffered with Liebschutz, but finally gave him his thirty dollars.

I broke up the volume, sold the Emerson pamphlets for twenty-five dollars apiece, and lay in wait with the broadside for Henry Wagner.

I fear my face was not altogether free of a smirk when I spread out the broadside before him. And I am sure I have never seen Wagner so mad as when he finally gave me a thousand dollars for one sheet of paper.

Mr. Wagner was not given to passing out free information if he thought it could ever be used against him. I have often wondered since whether he should have been annoyed that his parade of knowledge had cost him money, or gratified that it resulted in my finding the broadside at all.

I had a chance to feel this on my own hide fairly soon afterward. Henry Stevens of Vermont, a great antiquarian and a great bibliographer, founded a bookselling firm in London that is still in business. Their present American specialist, Roland Tree, is one of my close friends.

During my early visits to London they used to sell me Western and nineteenth-century Americana for very little money. I reciprocated by telling them everything I could think of about the new vogue for Western Americana and the books that were carrying it.

They in turn let me loose among the stacks on their labyrinthine third floor, which had obviously not been dusted for fifteen or twenty years. I spent several days doing what I hoped was cleaning them out of unusual Western items. As far as I could see, I left the shelves stripped.

Years later, Roland Tree, back from one of his visits to the London office, dropped in at my office and waved a copy of *Louis Tarascon* under my nose.

"How the hell did I miss that, Roly?" I asked. "I thought I cleaned you out."

"Well, we finally moved and dusted all the books on the third floor, and this had fallen down behind the shelves. You know, I think selling you that Western stuff cheap was one of the best investments we ever made."

Here is a double stumble, one by a discoverer and one by me.

Among the most interesting tales of Western exploration is James O. Pattie's *Narrative,* edited by Timothy Flint, one of the most remarkable and certainly the most active literary figure of his time in the Ohio Valley. For many years anyone who had a copy of the book, printed in Cincinnati in 1833, congratulated himself upon owning a rare first edition.

Then ten or fifteen years ago Mr. G. Y. Barber, the prominent collector, got hold of a defective copy with a title page dated Cincinnati, 1831. Being a wise man, he rushed straight to Wilberforce Eames at the New York Public Library.

Mr. Eames poked at all the copies of the 1833 edition that he could lay hands on. What he found was that each one had a "cancel title"—the original title page had been torn out and another one, dated 1833, had been bound in. This was an expedient resorted to now and then by the publisher of some spectacularly unsuccessful book, such as Thoreau's *A Week on the Concord and Merrimack Rivers.* Nearly all of the first edition would be left on the publisher's hands, so by changing the title pages he would try to give the impression that the book had run into a new edition.

After Mr. Eames's discovery, my little bit of luck is pretty tame, though it did not seem so to me at the time. While my son Tom and I were driving through the outskirts of Nice I spied a bookshop.

"Stop, Tom," I said.

"Oh, hell, you can't ever get past a junk shop, can you?" he replied, filially. He was quite right, too.

I asked the proprietor if he had any Americana. With a voluble flow of "*Oui, oui,*" he bowed us into the shop and produced three volumes. Two of them I have quite forgotten. The third was Pattie's *Narrative* with the 1831 title page.

This was one of the times when the French did not think the

franc could possibly fall any lower—I believe it was worth about three cents. Shrewd French dealers marked their merchandise in pounds; the Italians were using the Swiss francs. The price of three pounds for Pattie caused no difficulty, but the dealer spent nearly an hour desperately trying to translate that sum into francs so that I could give it to him.

(Absolutely the only difference between the 1831 and 1833 Patties, I might remark, is five hundred dollars.)

Three or four decades ago there were five librarians and three private collectors vying with one another for items of American poetry. Ten-cent doggerel became worth five, ten dollars, almost anything you wanted to ask. One of the rival librarians, a customer of mine, had charge of a large public institution in western New York. His board of trustees was getting uneasy about the amount of money he spent for such poetry. He asked me to attend a meeting and back him up. One of the trustees held under my nose a splendid ten-cent book that I had sold to them for $7.50. "Now, Mr. Everitt, don't you believe that we might have got this elsewhere for twenty-five cents?"

"How much do you pay your librarian?" I retorted.

"Five thousand a year."

"Well, if you want to give him six months and an expense account, I am morally certain that he could find you a copy for *ten* cents. Any other questions?"

The rarest piece of poetry I ever handled came to me through my invariable habit of never giving nor asking for a discount. I was wandering through Glasgow, looking for trouble, and passed a little shop with stamps and odds and ends in the window. I stopped in and asked my standard question, "Any Americana?"

The proprietor, a delightful Scotsman named Harrison, said he had this and that. I poked through the lot, found three or four pounds' worth, and laid my money on the line.

Harrison was so stunned by my not asking for a discount that he said, "Would you like me to keep an eye out for this sort of thing?"

I said I would be delighted, and never gave him another thought.

Two years later I wandered past his shop and turned in.

Sure enough, he had saved me a couple of dozen things. One was Samuel Groome's Quaker tract, *A Glass for the People of New England,* 1676, that Henry Stevens catalogued at two hundred and fifty pounds. Harrison had this marked thirty shillings.

I had hardly laid that in the "take" pile when I picked up a copy of Samuel Davies's *Miscellaneous Poems,* Williamsburg, Virginia, 1751. The bibliography of early American printed books by Charles Evans lists only the title from a newspaper advertisement, under 1752. This was the first time that an informed eye had ever looked on a copy.

"I'm sorry," said Harrison apologetically, "but I shall have to ask you ten bob for that."

"Oh, that's all right," I said. "Just put it in this pile here."

Up to that time, Dr. Harry Lyman Koopman of Brown University's library had made a proud boast that he never turned down any item of American poetry lacking in his collection. So when I got home I sent a quotation of $300 to his successors.

Dr. Koopman's successor replied, saying that they had adopted a new rule: no piece of poetry was worth more than $75.

I was digesting this information, to which I am afraid I

never replied, when Dr. Clarence S. Brigham of the American Antiquarian Society came in. I showed him my prize. "How much?"

"Three hundred."

"I'll take it, but I don't know when I'll pay for it." Pause. "I've got a better collection of American poetry than Koopman has, anyhow."

Some months later Dr. Brigham reported that he had found a second copy on the shelves of the Boston Public Library and a third at Princeton. It's the same old story: find one copy of an unknown item and the rest start coming out of hiding.

While Adolph Stager and I were thriving on the American poetry boom, we accumulated a huge lot of duplicates. Finally, in a frantic effort to find a new customer or two and clear our shelves, we put out a catalogue listing over three thousand items of American poetry.

For three weeks there was not a sound. We began to wonder if our errand boy, like the famous colored maid, had mailed the catalogues in a receptacle plainly marked "Deposit Litter Here."

And then came a copy of the catalogue with twelve hundred items checked, and a note from the Huntington Library: "We will take all of these if we may have a 15 per cent discount."

The one inviolable rule on which Stager and I had done business was, as I have just mentioned, no discount to anyone. Our colleagues in the trade were allowed 10 per cent; everyone else paid the marked price.

In this particular case rules sagged a little; it wasn't the principle of the thing, it was the money.

I once put a note in one of my catalogues to the effect that I was not honest enough to give discounts. If I am cataloguing a $5 book, and know I shall have to give a discount (I wrote), I automatically list it at $7.50, so the discount buyer loses in the end.

Probably everyone has tried to get a discount at some time in his life, but some people always try. In the course of years I got increasingly fed up with horse-collared gentry who would ask sanctimoniously for a clerical discount. Finally, when a clergyman asked for a clerical discount on three volumes off the three-for-a-quarter table, my patience gave way.

"Hell, no," I exploded. "I wouldn't even take your check!"

I have mentioned the Samuel Groome Quaker tract. Rather inappropriately, Quaker items are a terrific game of chance. Nine tenths of them are trash; the remnant are so scarce they make your hair stand on end. Or at least they seem so until you get into the swing of it. For instance, I had read the advance proofs of the Stevens catalogue, showing a reproduction of the Groome title page. That put me on the lookout, and I was ready to grab Harrison's copy.

Then, very shortly afterward, an old lady came to my office at Dauber & Pine's with a bundle of Quaker tracts. She said that the American Art Association had told her they were worthless, but that Everitt would give her five dollars for the lot. She said she would be very glad if I could do that.

Nearly all her whole lot were among the hair-raising remnant of Quaker publications, and one was a Groome. I said no, I could not give her five dollars because they were worth much more than that, but I could give her forty-five. To cut a long story short, within two years of my seeing the Stevens catalogue I turned up a total of seven copies of Groome, which I sold to various collectors for a good deal less than Stevens's price, but still at nice round figures.

Then I found an eighth copy. The peculiarity of this one

was that it had an errata list. None of the others had any such list.

I compared the mistakes with the copies I had sold and discovered that all the changes had been made, so that no errata list was necessary. Or, to put it crassly, all the copies sold up to then were second editions.

Somehow or other, this first edition with errata list disappeared, and I am morally certain it is not to be found in any collection I know of.

If we leave out first editions of fiction, which are largely a matter of momentary whim among collectors, fashions in collecting Americana have a special peculiarity: for thirty or fifty or a hundred years you simply can't give away books on a subject; then a craze for that subject arises, and you simply can't find the books. Fashions in Americana wear out, not, as most fashions do, because people get tired of the subject, but because a brisk demand for a very tiny supply pushes prices beyond what any ordinary buyer can pay. In my time, for instance, I have seen the craze for Washington material reach the sky and come tumbling down. I don't expect it to climb again, simply because there is too wide a variety available.

At the height of the Washington fashion, there were at least twenty-five well-heeled collectors trying to get copies of all the engraved portraits ever published of Washington. The leader in the race was Hampton L. Carson of Philadelphia.

One day an answer to one of my advertisements in a Norfolk, Virginia, paper took me to a Negro hovel so filthy and rickety that for almost the only time in my life I was really scared. On the second floor were two or three hundred old schoolbooks. They were so covered with filth that I dreaded to touch them. I had to get out of the place somehow, so I hastily opened two or three volumes. In one of them was a small copper engraving of a portrait bust of Washington, signed by Wright. Holding my nose, I proffered a quarter for it as the quickest means of escape. My tender was accepted, and I slid the engraving into my breast pocket, where it was no larger than my wallet.

A portrait engraver named Max Rosenthal was Mr. Carson's agent in buying Washington portraits. He dropped into my store one day, and all I could show him was my tiny copper-plate engraving. He made the inexcusable mistake of letting his eyes light up at the sight. He didn't like me, and I didn't like him, so instead of asking two dollars and settling for a dollar I said, "Max, that will cost you three hundred and fifty."

I was stunned when he said. "I can only give you three hundred."

"You bought it," said I.

He was not far wrong, as things went then. In the Carson auction my print brought $450.

A few weeks ago, in 1950, I declined with thanks an opportunity to buy another copy for ten dollars.

Washington is a case of oversupply. Some rarities are in very short supply, but in even shorter demand.

Two things that every American autograph collector wants are a set of the signers of the Declaration of Independence and a set of the presidents on White House stationery. You can assemble a set of signers without too much trouble if you have the price. You can also get a set of the presidents—except for William Henry Harrison, who died after one month in office. No amount of money that you are ever likely to see will tempt one of those Harrison autographs out of hiding.

Two signers of the Declaration of Independence whom you will have to dig down for are Button Gwinnett and Thomas

Lynch, Jr. Twenty years ago there was a flurry of publicity about the fabulous value of Gwinnett signatures, and Dr. Rosenbach bought one for $38,000. I am inclined to think he also had another one in stock. Later Henry Stevens, III, brought me a schoolbook containing an unquestionably genuine Gwinnett autograph. (I think the main reason Gwinnett's autographs are so scarce is that he never got much beyond the elementary schoolbook level as a penman. No letter of his has ever been discovered.) "Charlie," said Stevens, "maybe we can both make some money. I see Rosy just paid thirty-eight thousand for one of these."

I took the book to Mitchell Kennerley, the head of the Anderson Galleries. "This is beautiful," he told me, "but it's no use. I can't put this in a sale unless Dr. Rosenbach says it's authentic."

Although both of us thought he'd be willing to do it, we didn't quite have the nerve to ask for authentication from a man who already owned two high-priced copies. The best authentication in my mind was the fact that Stevens had paid a shilling for the book – not enough money to justify much trouble in forging it.

I had to send the book back to London.

While I was working for Dauber & Pine, a man dressed like a laborer offered me a contemporary almanac with the name Button Gwinnett written on it. It didn't look at all like the one on Henry Stevens's book, so I said no thank you.

A day or two later came a telephone call from Frank Bender, a Fourth Avenue dealer. "Charlie, I've hit the jackpot. I just gave a guy two dollars for an almanac with the signatures of Button Gwinnett *and* Thomas Lynch on the front."

"Frank," I said, "the last time I saw it, it was only worth half as much; it didn't have the signature of Lynch on it yet."

PART II

The Consumers

1. Who Buys Americana?

YOU MAY be a trifle startled to know that I am not much interested in collectors. I have known fewer than a dozen real ones in my sixty years of hunting rare Americana. Most of the people who smirk bashfully and admit they are collectors are really speculators.

Take two good examples of thirty or forty years ago. Jacob Chester Chamberlain was the outstanding collector of American first editions of his day. Mr. Chamberlain was a true collector: he cared only for books, not at all for their value in dollars. I once sold him a copy of Hawthorne's first book, *Fanshawe,* although he already had two good copies. Mine was an eighth of an inch taller than either, and this point made the book worth buying to Mr. Chamberlain, without much regard to the price.

Mr. Chamberlain never questioned a bookseller's price, and at least in my own experience he never passed up a book he wanted because of the tag on it. Once in a while he might say to me, "I'm a bit overbought. Do you mind if I take sixty days to pay you?"

One of many happy experiences I had with Mr. Chamberlain involved the famous Troutbeck House near Amenia, New York, which once belonged to Marvin Benton. Benton was an intimate friend of the great New England authors, particularly Thoreau and Emerson. After his death, his heir, his brother Joel, took me up to look over the library.

What I found was several hundred volumes of our greatest midnineteenth-century authors, with long, intimate presentation inscriptions to Mr. Benton.

My usual attitude toward inscribed copies is best shown by the way I catalogued an autographed copy of George W. Childs's *Recollections*. I listed it at $1.50, with the note: "I make a standing offer of $2.50 for any copy of this book not inscribed by the author." Benton's books were something else: the inscriptions gave them a life of their own beyond what was on the printed page. I wanted Mr. Chamberlain to have those volumes.

Jolting up to Amenia on the Harlem Railroad, I had taken the precaution of consulting my bank book, which showed a balance of $375. I cannot say it was without a qualm that I offered Mr. Joel Benton $3750 that afternoon for his brother's books. He promptly accepted, and there I was.

I asked for the use of his telephone and got hold of Mr. Chamberlain. I told him my fix, told him he had to have some of the books, and asked what I was to do next.

"Write him a check," said Mr. Chamberlain, "and I'll cover it at your bank in the morning."

When Mr. Chamberlain and I came to settle accounts, I offered him his choice, at his own price, among the 2200 odd volumes I had brought back from Amenia.

He picked out seventy-one and said, "There. I'm satisfied if you are." I feel perfectly certain that the last thing in the world he knew or cared about was the fact that fifty of those volumes were one day to bring just over four thousand dollars at auction.

I had fun buying the copy of *Fanshawe* that I sold to Mr. Chamberlain. My wife and I both come from Orange County, New York, and old Judge Beattie once laid down a ruling that no book could be sold in Orange County until I had passed on it. The Judge tipped me off to a household auction that was being held at Monroe, New York. The auction bill read: SALE RAIN OR SHINE. I did not know whether this covered the blizzard that was going on that morning, but I took a chance. Very few other buyers were as grave as I, and none of these showed any interest in the books except one man, Pliny Earle, the millionaire painter. He had a large mansion on the mountain near Monroe.

When the auctioneer got around to the book, he held up two plump volumes and said, as country auctioneers always do, "Here we have some real old books, maybe first editions, printed way back in the 1800's." Mr. Earle's eyes brightened.

I don't know whether mine did; they were bright enough already to see that the books were a set of an American edition of Josephus, which any self-respecting bookseller would be ashamed to expose on his ten-cent table.

I dropped out of the bidding in time so that Mr. Earle did not have to pay over fifteen dollars for the set.

The auctioneer began to think there must be something to this book business, and he proudly displayed a set of Rollin's *Ancient History*, which is normally worth almost as much as a fair Josephus. The difference was reflected in the price at which I relinquished the Rollin to Mr. Earle – $2.50.

Like most millionaires, Mr. Earle was careful of his money,

and he came over for a word with me. "It strikes me books are selling pretty high today," he said.

"If you'll go over in that corner and sit down and shut up," I told him, "I'll make you a present of every goddamned book in the house except one."

The auctioneer now found books a drug on the market. Nobody would bid on individual items, so he finally had to put up the remaining 340 volumes as a lot. He started calling for a fifty-dollar bid. Silence. Forty. Silence. Thirty. Silence.

When he got down to five, I yelled, "I'll give you three-fifty!"

"Sold," said the auctioneer, banging his hammer.

I fished my one book, the copy of *Fanshawe,* out of the pile, then paid my bill and handed the receipt to Mr. Earle. This left the trucking bill on him.

While I was killing time waiting for my train, the auctioneer put up a large and very beautiful silver luster cake dish. "This is not solid silver," he explained conscientiously; "this is plated ware." He swallowed when I opened with a five-dollar bid. I think he was too surprised even to swallow when Mr. Earle finally carried the dish off for $125.

A little later all the family flat silver was put up, and this time my opening bid of five dollars was successful. I went trudging down to the depot, walking lopsided, with *Fanshawe* in my right coat pocket and some seventy-five pounds of solid silver in an old telescopic bag in my left hand.

Mr. Chamberlain got the *Fanshawe* for $750, and Mr. Gorham got the silver for $350.

Among collectors at the opposite pole from Mr. Chamberlain was William Harris Arnold, whose eminence among collectors of English first editions equaled that of Mr. Chamberlain among American books. Mr. Arnold never paid me

$100 for a book without first asking himself if he could get $200 for it ten years later, and very seldom without asking me if I couldn't let it go for $75. In fact, he seemed more interested in discounts than in books.

Mr. Arnold was unique in that he issued a very fancily printed volume showing the price he paid for each item in his collection, set against the price it brought when he ended his collecting career with an auction. So far as I could see, the underlying purpose, conscious or unconscious, of this listing was to show how much cleverer Mr. Arnold was than the dealers in rare books who had supplied him.

Actually the list was somewhat misleading because it took no account of overhead or selling cost. Mr. Arnold should really have known better than this: by profession he was the buyer for H. B. Claflin, the largest book wholesaler America has ever known.

Mr. Arnold's figures say one thing, but my calculations seem to show another, which is that, all things considered, he just about got his money back. He certainly did not make any fancy profit.

In fact, my favorite axiom is that any rare bookseller will happily pay for a taxi to bring a speculator into his store.

The late A. Edward Newton is justly famous for his *The Amenities of Book Collecting,* the most charming volume ever written on this subject. Nevertheless he was a prince among speculators. In a later volume he tried to talk about rare-book prices, and his misinformation cost the collectors among his devout following many hundreds of thousands of dollars.

His nisinformation was due sometimes to what Dr. Johnson called "Ignorance, madam, pure ignorance," and sometimes to obstinacy. In one of his books he casually remarked that a first edition of *Huckleberry Finn* in blue cloth was worth many times as much as one in green cloth. This I presume was ignorance.

Shortly afterward I showed him a canvasser's prospectus from the American Publishing Company of Hartford, dated 1884, which said that the forthcoming *Huckleberry Finn* was to be issued in green cloth but that it would also be available in blue for purchasers wishing copies uniform with *Tom Sawyer.* Mr. Newton never revised his original statement that the blue had priority.

Although I am quite conscious of being an old crank, I must remark that I am not wholly alone in my strictures on Mr. Newton. Among the most famous bibliographers of early medical books were Mr. and Mrs. Leroy Crummer. Take a look some time at *A Catalogue of Mss. and Medical Books Printed before 1640,* Omaha, 1927. Mrs. Crummer was known and loved by everyone in the old-book world.

Scene: E. Joseph's in London at 10:30 A.M.; Sam Joseph at desk. Enter Mrs. Crummer: "Sam, I just must have a drink. I spent about the most horrible evening of my life last night."

C.P.E. (butting in): "You must have been out to dinner with A. Edward Newton."

Mrs. Crummer: "How did you guess? Even worse, Gabriel Wells was there. What a hellish three hours! Nothing but 'I bought a copy of this for so much: it's worth so much.' "

The final sale of Mr. Newton's collection was an example of what usually happens to speculators. Mr. Newton himself expressed the opinion that his collection would bring over a million. A professional appraiser put the figure at $750,000. I, being completely ignorant of the kind of books Mr. Newton collected, had made a guess of $250,000.

The sale, naturally, was the towering event of the auction season. I have heard that the catalogues and publicity cost

$50,000. Booksellers and Mr. Newton's admirers on both sides of the Atlantic talked of little else for weeks beforehand.

When the auctioneer's hammer fell on the last lot, the total take was around $300,000. This might have been bigger if the auction cataloguer had not withdrawn several of Mr. Newton's most famous items, which were discovered not to be what Mr. Newton assumed they were.

As it was, the devout Newtonians, who made what prices there were, would probably discover, upon trying to resell their treasures, that they would not fetch a fifth of what they had brought at the Newton sale. This is one more proof that speculators get stuck in the long run. I hope most of the buyers at the Newton sale (who were, incidentally very largely unknown to the booksellers) were like the Midwestern man who wired me to place bids of thirty dollars each on some volumes of Conrad. I went down to the exhibition, and then telephoned to my client that he would be ashamed to have such bad copies on his shelves. "Hell," he said, "I don't want the books; I want the bookplates."

Sometimes, though, speculators are right. Some years ago one of them was in my store and told me he was considering buying a first edition of Cooper's *The Last of the Mohicans* in Boston for two hundred dollars.

"Joe," I said, "don't be a damn fool. I'll get you one for less than a hundred."

"Charlie, you're always bluffing," was his reply to my kind offer. He then left for his office.

Within three hours a scout friend of mine marched in with the most beautiful set that has ever been seen to this day. The paper labels looked as if they had just come from the bindery.

"Twelve-fifty," said the scout, timidly.

I pursued my speculator by telephone, and he hurried back to the store. His eyes bulged.

"To you, thirty-seven-fifty," I said.

A few months later, in a moment of financial stress, my friend decided to realize on his American first editions. When I saw my *Last of the Mohicans* sell for $3250, I began to wish I had not been so sensitive about being called a bluffer.

I put out my first catalogue in October, 1898. My first two customers, no relation to each other, were Paul Leicester Ford and James Ford of the United States Rubber Company.

Paul Ford came from a wealthy family of book collectors and bibliographers; his father had probably the finest library in Brooklyn at the time. Paul was a hunchback, a famous popular novelist, author of *Janice Meredith* and other best sellers. For all his money and background, he was undoubtedly the meanest buyer I have ever contended with. Apparently Paul inherited this trait from his father, because my friend Alexander Thompson, who was studying law on nothing a year, once went there for dinner. Mr. Ford, Sr., said very earnestly, "Alec, come over and use the library any time you want." Slight pause. "Of course Paul will expect a little something for showing you around."

James Ford, on the other hand, valued his time more than his money. His first visit to me was for the purpose of inspecting a copy of the first report of the Delaware, Lackawanna and Western Railroad, priced at fifteen dollars. "Don't you think I might buy this somewhere else for less?" he asked me.

"I imagine so," I said. "I paid a quarter for it."

"But don't you think maybe I'd save time by giving you the fifteen?" he asked with a twinkle.

When Marshall Saville and Dr. Frederick Hodge were leaving the Museum of the American Indian (Heye Foundation), Mr. Heye asked me to set a price on their private libraries, for acquisition by the museum. I appraised the Saville library at $50,000 and the Hodge library at $25,000.

When I told Mr. Heye the result, he said, "Now you go on down to Mr. Ford and get the money."

He made an eleven o'clock appointment for me with Mr. Ford for the following day. As I was going out of the door, Heye called after me, "Don't get there at 11:01 or 10:59; get there at eleven." I stood around, watching the hands of my watch for a couple of minutes before I announced myself to Mr. Ford's secretary.

"Mr. Ford," I greeted him, "George Heye wants seventy-five thousand to buy the Saville and Hodge collections."

"Are they worth it?"

"It was my appraisal."

"Do you want a check or a bond?" Then he added, "You picked a good day to come. I made a little money yesterday. And I don't mean just two or three hundred thousand dollars."

I have hardly ever known anyone who took such pleasure in giving away books. Mr. Ford was very generous to the library of the Museum of the American Indian, and the library of the Explorers' Club owed its existence almost entirely to him. He was the honorary president of the Explorers' Club, though his asthma prevented him from acting, and whenever anyone mentioned an important set of books that the library lacked, Mr. Ford would lean over to me and ask, "How much?" This was invariably followed by, "Get it, and send the bill to me."

Once when I was the chairman of the Explorers' Club library committee, someone mentioned a publication of the

Champlain Society, Mr. Ford went through his usual routine, and I told him the set would cost $250 or $300. I found a set in London and bought it for $250, but when I got back, Mr. Ford was dead. We held a meeting of the department heads of the club, nine in all, George Heye presiding. "This is a beautiful set," Mr. Heye said, "but all we can do is to send it back, because we haven't any money."

"I'd be glad to get it at that price," I said. "But how about this: suppose each of us kicks in twenty-five dollars, and you put up fifty, then we'll be able to keep the set."

They were all too shocked to say no.

Certainly no more genial or generous collector than William F. Gable, of Altoona, Pennsylvania, has lived during the past half century. He was known to every dealer, every important collector, every professional book-hunting "scout." He bought thousands of volumes that he did not want simply because he thought the dealers needed the money.

The last time I dined with him, at the old Belmont in New York, he told me that in a city like Altoona anyone who owned more than ten books was considered queer. A business acquaintance said to him at lunch, "Gable, I hear you have some nice books. Why don't you come over to dinner some evening and bring your books along? My wife is a great reader."

"I wondered what his wife would do," Gable told me, "if I appeared with twenty-two thousand books."

The auctioneer who catalogued and sold those books after Mr. Gable's death should have been drawn and quartered, preferably before he did the job. If any modern collector should happen on a priced catalogue from the Gable auction, I doubt whether he would buy another book. Hundreds upon hundreds of the association volumes Mr. Gable loved so much were sold to a dealer practically as wastepaper.

One of my favorite customers and friends for many years was Reverend Thomas R. Slicer, the pastor of the Unitarian Church at 20th Street and Fourth Avenue. Its red and black brick gave it the name of the Beefsteak Church. (Incidentally, I have never forgotten the time when Mr. Slicer announced a sermon on the Virgin Birth. The congregation, naturally, were all agog. He had a splendid pulpit presence, and he rose and calmly gave a text, not from the Bible, but from Browning. Then he leaned confidentially toward his flock. "What difference does it make? That's all I have to say about the Virgin Birth.")

I published a bibliography of Shelley, compiled by Mr. Slicer on the basis of the Harry B. Smith collection. He and I had an agreement that if any royalties came due, they were to be spent on a dinner at Dorlan's.

One banner year he earned $28. To spend such a huge amount, we had to invite two guests, both of them prominent members of Mr. Slicer's church.

A few days before, Mr. Slicer had picked up in a bookstore run by a man named Hamilton, at 38th Street and Third Avenue, a first edition of *Leaves of Grass,* priced at one dollar. Our guests, being active churchmen, felt uncomfortable about the ethics of this purchase. The book, even then, forty years ago, was worth around $350 (I have seen the time since when it would have brought $1500).

"Oh," I said, "don't give it another thought. Hamilton probably made ninety cents on the deal anyway."

This led one of the guests to ask what percentage rare-book dealers usually work on.

"I don't know about the rest of them," Mr. Slicer put in, "but Charlie doesn't work on percentages; he just works on straight larceny."

Later Mr. Slicer's health failed, and I got an unhappy telephone call from Mrs. Slicer, who said they were going to have to sell the books. Mr. Slicer was sick in bed, and to keep the news from him, she wanted me to inspect the library, but not to give away my presence by smoking.

I was familiar enough with Mr. Slicer's books so that it took me very little time to set a figure of five thousand as the amount they ought to bring.

As I started to leave, the maid said, "If you can spare a minute, Mr. Slicer would like to see you."

Up on the third floor of the brownstone house Mr. Slicer greeted me. "Well, Charlie, I've still got pretty good ears, I hear they want to sell my books. You'll find a good cigar on the mantel."

We sat and swapped stories about books for a while, and then I departed.

A few days later the name Slicer caught my eye on the obituary page of the paper. Mrs. Slicer had dropped dead. After that, Mr. Slicer moved to a hotel. As part of the moving, I got his books packed and shipped to the American Art Association for auctioning.

Two or three months later Mr. Slicer's nurse called and said that he had lost his voice; he was sinking, and hoped I might be able to call.

When I arrived in his hotel room, he drew me down within range of his voice. "I can't talk much any more, Charlie," he said, "so I thought I'd ask you to tell me a few stories. But first I want it to go on record that you are probably the worst appraiser that ever lived. You appraised my books at five thousand, and all they brought at auction was forty-nine hundred."

Three or four days later he was gone.

Book collectors who have a tinge of speculation in the blood often think they would make good booksellers. Sometimes they do. Ernest Wessen, of the Midland Rare Book Company, started as a collector, and is now one of the great dealers in this country. His catalogues over the last ten years have been without exception the most interesting ones issued in America. Probably there are not a dozen complete files of his catalogues in existence, one of them mine. If Mr. Wessen ever issues an index, it will be by far the best bibliography ever printed on the Midwest.

Seymour Dunbar was an ink-slinger from way back; he loved books, wrote several, including the unique *History of Travel in America,* and made various collections to help in his writing. When my lifelong friend Edward Eberstadt set up in the business of dealing in Western Americana, he put a sign on his door: SEYMOUR DUNBAR, BUYER. Dunbar was also the cataloguer for the concern.

In one of Eberstadt's first catalogues, Dunbar devoted a page of glowing description to John Gilmary Shea's *History of the Catholic Church in America.* He put on a $65 price.

I called up to jeer at Ed Eberstadt because the set was in print for ten dollars.

A week later he called back to jeer at me because he had seven orders at $65 each.

(This proves that there are always at least seven librarians who do not look up the U.S. Catalogue before they place an order.)

Dunbar's first big killing as a buyer was of himself. A

storage warehouse called up, and Dun went over. In the middle of the evening he came back and reported to Eberstadt that they had just made a fortune.

"How did we do it?" asked Eberstadt.

"Well, it was pretty dark in the warehouse, and I couldn't see much, but there were at least five hundred big volumes, and I got the man to take five hundred for the lot," he said.

Eberstadt went over in daylight to look at the books and meet the owner. The unkindly sun revealed a display of *Turner Art Gallery, German Art, Encyclopaedia Britannica,* ninth edition, and similar gems. Eberstadt shuddered as he said he didn't want the books.

"But Mr. Dunbar is your buyer," the owner insisted, "and he offered me five hundred."

"I'm a good fellow," said Eberstadt. "I'll give you a hundred if I don't have to take the books."

"Five hundred," the owner persisted.

"Two hundred, and you keep the books," said Eberstadt.

"Five hundred."

"Three hundred, and no removals," said Eberstadt.

"Five hundred."

"Four hundred, and you keep them."

"Five hundred."

"All right, damn it, five hundred, but I positively will not take the books."

When Seymour Dunbar went to the office the next morning, the sign read: EDWARD EBERSTADT, RARE WESTERN BOOKS.

On two occasions customers of mine have bitten off more than they could chew; one of them fought on to the bitter end, the other cried quits.

Shortly after the Lincoln automobile came on the market,

I had a letter from Henry M. Leland, its manufacturer, simply saying, "Send me a copy of every book that mentions Abraham Lincoln."

I wrote back, cautious as always, that there was a considerable number of such books, and did he really want them all?

He sent back my letter with a message scrawled across the face: "Can't you read English?"

In the course of the next three weeks I sent him thirteen cases of books. Check by return mail.

During the next six months I sent six more cases. All checks by return mail.

A few months after that, I sent him a shipment amounting to $1082.

A day or two later I read in the paper that the Lincoln Motor Car Company had folded and that Henry Ford had got hold of it.

Well, I thought, I made enough on the other nineteen cases to cover this lot.

The very next morning brought an envelope with Mr. Leland's personal check for $1082.

(It was just about this time that Mrs. Henry Ford's secretary wrote to ask if I could supply a copy of a scarce seventeenth-century French cook book. I spent some twenty dollars advertising for it in the London and Paris trade journals, and at long last got a quotation from Paris at fifty. Wanting to make a good impression on such a prized prospective customer, I wrote to say that Mrs. Ford could have the book for seventy-five. After a delay the secretary replied that Mrs. Ford wondered whether I could not get the book photostated for less money.)

My other overenterprising customer was Ambassador Walter Hines Page, then a partner in the book publishing firm of Doubleday and McClure. Mr. Page's order to me read: "We propose to publish the finest encyclopedia ever compiled. Please send me two sets of every edition of every encyclopedia ever published in any language, for the use of our editorial department."

I called him up. "Mr. Page, you know you're ordering quite a lot of encyclopedias."

His reply was apparently the conventional one for such occasions: "Can't you read English?"

In the first six months I sent him three tons of encyclopedias. The next six months yielded only two more tons. I was just contemplating further tonnage when my phone rang: "This is Walter Page. Stop!" If I had not been so rudely interrupted in my shipment, Mr. Page might ultimately have assembled enough encyclopedias to finish his task; but as it was, the Doubleday and McClure encyclopedia never appeared.

Despite the rarity of certain Williamsburg imprints and despite the fine English collections of persons like William Byrd, of Westover, and George Washington, southeastern books are pretty slim pickings, and Southern collectors are even scarcer than the books. In the city of Lynchburg, Virginia, for instance, the only book collector I ever heard of was the cashier of a local bank. He thought, perhaps correctly but anyhow illegally, that his need was greater than the bank's, whereupon the bank got a chattel mortgage for several thousand dollars on his library and threw him in jail.

Senator Carter Glass's secretary, Mrs. Martha Adams, with whom I had a good deal of correspondence, wrote to me about this, and I came down for a look at the library.

The bank directors finally decided to accept my offer of

20 per cent of the chattel mortgage, which, I may add, was a damn good price.

During this stay in Lynchburg I had my first meeting with Senator Glass, one of the few great statesmen who have been in the United States Senate within my lifetime. On my next-to-last day in Lynchburg, Mrs. Adams took me over to see two decayed Southern gentlewomen who had some books. As we were driving over, she said, "You've simply got to spend ten dollars because I'm sure these poor things haven't eaten in three days."

I promptly pounced on three items from the near end of a shelf, peeled off a sawbuck, and made good my escape. On the way to the railroad station, I heaved the books into a convenient vacant lot.

Before long I had a quavery letter from one of the indigent gentlewomen, saying they had been unable to sleep, and could I please let them have the books back, as they had belonged to Father.

I was constrained to write a letter of explanation, in which I pointed out that on my high-pressure buying trips I would come back with many thousands of volumes, and it might be months before I could uncover the ones they wanted. I have sometimes wondered what a truly ethical bookseller would have done in my situation.

Lynchburg had only one collector, and he was in jail. Roanoke had three: Jack Hancock; Ed Stone, the state printer; and Julius B. Fishburn of the local newspaper.

On my frequent trips to stay with Hancock, I got to know the other two as well. Ed Stone, naturally enough, was interested in examples of the work of famous printers. He did not care particularly whether he had the entire book; a couple of pages would do.

About this time there was a great flutter over a character named Dr. Otto Vollbehr, a German who was willing, as a charitable enterprise, to sell his collection of incunabula to the United States Government for a million dollars. As a matter of fact, Vollbehr had peddled his collection all over hell; nobody in New York, Philadelphia, Boston, or Chicago, dealers, collectors, or librarians, would give him his minimum figure of $250,000.

Then a tidal wave of publicity somehow got into motion, all about this fabulous collection and the unique opportunity for the United States to acquire it, how generous it was of the kind Dr. Vollbehr, and so on and so on. As a result, when someone introduced a bill to buy the Vollbehr collection for $750,000, it passed practically without a dissenting voice; any senator or congressman who voted against it felt himself a boor and an ignoramus.

About this time I was in Lynchburg, and my old friend Mrs. Adams told me the Senator was at liberty in his office at the newspaper if I would like to see him. By way of making conversation, he said, "Everitt, you may be interested to know that I was instrumental in getting the Vollbehr Collection for the Library of Congress."

"I'm always interested in anything you do, Senator," I said. "Tell me this: who split the five hundred thousand?"

Senator Glass blushed slightly, then said, "Tell me about it."

"Well, Senator, it seems to me that when something is offered at two hundred fifty thousand for two years with no takers, and then the Library of Congress suddenly decides to pay seven hundred and fifty thousand, somebody should be entitled to a commission."

He grinned. "I bet you know who got me into it."

"Sure," I said. "Ed Stone, who thinks any book two hundred years old is worth two hundred dollars."

One day an extremely dapper gentleman came into my 34th Street store and asked if I had anything on Louisiana. I said I had a few things, and produced them.

He looked them over. "What's the discount?"

"Sorry," I said. "That word isn't in my dictionary."

He looked rather taken aback, and finally handed me a business card: Sidney Swartz, president, Maison Blanche, Canal Street, New Orleans.

We parted on good terms, without doing any business.

In a day or two he came down from the Ambassador Hotel. "What became of those Louisiana books you showed me?"

"Here they are."

He wrote out a check, then handed me a cylindrical package.

"What's this, Mr. Swartz?"

"Well, you're the only bookseller in New York that doesn't give me a discount, and I'm beginning to suspect your books are worth what you say they are. So I thought I'd give you the best umbrella I could find. If you're ever in New Orleans, drop in; we'll do some business."

A year or so after this I got tired of my quiet life and took a boat for the Gulf. At New Orleans one of my first calls was at the Maison Blanche. On the third floor I found a huge bronze gate, guarded by a secretary.

"Could I see Mr. Swartz?" I asked.

"Have you an appointment?"

"Sorry, no."

"Well, in that case it will take about three days to see Mr. Swartz."

"Are you Miss Delaney?" I inquired, forewarned by Swartz's stories.

"Well, yes, since you ask. Might I ask your name?"

"I'm Charlie Everitt."

"Hell, why didn't you say so? Walk right in."

In I walked, to find Swartz, a Catholic priest, and a reporter seated at a desk bearing five assorted bottles of whisky. Swartz glanced up quickly. "Say, you fellows, get the hell out. I want to talk to Charlie."

After a certain amount of book chat, Swartz said, "I'm going to take you down to Cusack's house. He's a fur dealer. He used to be president of the Louisiana Historical Society, only he had a fight with them."

Cusack's house proved to be a residence of some forty rooms, none of which bore any traces of a duster within living memory. The visit was passed entirely in civilities. As we were leaving, Mr. Cusack said, "Mr. Everitt, I'm thinking of selling my library. Could you get down here at eight tomorrow morning?"

The next morning he came straight to the point. "I don't like Swartz, and I don't like any American bookseller. Every soul in Louisiana has double-crossed me at one time or another. What I want to do now is this. You can take any book out of my library that you please, and tell me what you'll pay for it. I'll write the figure on a sheet of paper. Then we'll see."

After two days of this he had some forty sheets closely covered with figures. He tried to strike a total; I was no help because addition is one art that I have never learned. Finally he called his sons, and they tried.

"Well," said Mr. Cusack, "let's take an average of these four different totals." The result of this calculation was $5247.

Then the boys took me outside to look for shipping containers.

The chief thing I discovered in this search was a decrepit old shed, one collapsing corner of which was propped up by a flat leather-backed volume marked "Music."

I got one of the boys to hold up that corner of the shed while I removed the book. The shed then fell down in a cloud of dust.

"Mr. Cusack," I said, "you can add one hundred dollars to the total for this."

He said, "If I'm fool enough to prop up a shed with hundred-dollar books, I can't make you pay for them. It's yours."

The "Music" consisted of 181 pieces of Confederate sheet music, and Mr. Wallace Cathcart of the Western Reserve Historical Society library was delighted at the chance to pay me $250 for it.

I was studying a catalogue from Francis Edwards of London one day when a man came into the store and wanted a first edition of Arthur Young's *Travels in France.* This, of course, is the book that did more than any other one thing to develop and improve European agriculture.

I said I had no set but suggested that he buy this one from London out of Francis Edwards's catalogue.

The inquirer asked permission to use my telephone. As it was right at my elbow, I could not help overhearing.

He said, "Please phone the London office and have them send a man over to this address with ten pounds and get this set of books. Then call me back here."

Thirty-five minutes later my telephone rang, to report that the complete writings of Arthur Young were in my new acquaintance's London office.

"What do I owe you?" he asked.

"Oh, what are you talking about? Who are you, anyway?"

He gave me his card: Orlando Webber. Later, after he became a steady customer, I discovered that he had probably the finest collection in the country on economics, and certainly the best lot of American Colonial pamphlets.

Mr. Webber would take a fancy to certain titles, such as J. S. Gibbons's *The Banks of New York,* a good fifty-cent book, and would buy every copy he could lay hands on to give away to his friends. During his lifetime he ran the price of Gibbons up to five dollars. (It is back now to $1.50.)

Another of his favorites was Colwell's *Ways and Means of Payment.* When he started buying the book, it was fairly common, but as a result of his campaign I have not seen one in the past ten years.

I was very fond of Dan Beard, for many, many years the chief scout executive of the Boy Scouts of America. He could eat more mince pie and throw a tomahawk better than anyone I ever heard of, and he also did more for the kids of America than anyone I have ever known. Although perhaps they did not realize it, the kids showed their gratitude, because his *Boy's Handbook* supported him all his life. It still sells in large quantities.

Once when he was living in Flushing, Long Island, I went over to see him. Mrs. Beard had just bought a large light-blue English platter. She was quite boastful about it.

I said, "Mrs. Beard, do you know the difference between the light-blue and dark-blue English platters?"

"No," she said.

"Well, you do know that the English lords and ladies used to eat at the same table with their servants."

"Yes, I had heard about that."

"Well, to make sure they never mixed up the plates, they had dark blue for themselves, and light blue for the servants."

Dan Beard told me later that he never saw that light-blue platter again.

Everyone remembers Dan Beard as the grand old man of scouting. Not so many remember that he began life as an illustrator. One of his most important commissions was the job of illustrating Mark Twain's *A Connecticut Yankee in King Arthur's Court.*

I once had a copy of the book in which Dan Beard had marked the names of the originals of all the drawings. The only ones I remember are Merlin, who was drawn from Alfred, Lord Tennyson, and the pig, who was drawn from Queen Victoria.

Not long before his death, Mr. Beard called me over to appraise his books and pictures. He had a very fine collection of costume prints, a splendid lot of autographs, a lot of standard books relating to American Indians and the West, and many sets of his own drawings. In the case of the Mark Twain illustrations, there was usually a letter from the author attached, in most cases heartily approving the drawing but sometimes suggesting a slight change.

Mr. Beard told me he intended to give the costume prints to Cooper Union and the autographs and original drawings to his club in New York, and he wanted to sell the books. He repeated this conversation at dinner in the presence of his wife and daughter, adding that I was to have the disposal of his literary property.

His death was quickly followed by the announcement of an auction at the Kende Galleries. What became of his prints and autographs I never knew. When I inspected the stuff at the auction, I found that Gimbel Brothers' expert cataloguer had offered the items in broken sets and miscellaneous bundles which, in my opinion, made it difficult for any reasonable buyer. The collection brought less than 20 per cent of my appraisal.

This was just one of the many instances that have proved to me that both executors and widows regard any book collection with suspicion and contempt.

I happened to spend one summer in Port Washington, Long Island, and by way of amusement I ran an ad for two months, announcing that I bought old books. Not a single reply came in.

Five blocks from where I was, John C. Irving, Washington Irving's nephew, had lived. The descendants paid a Roslyn antique dealer seventy-five cents to remove the books. That same summer I paid him two thousand dollars for a small part of his haul. (Of course I doubled or tripled my money within the next two or three months — the kind of cheap summer vacation I always try for.)

Speaking of Irving, his *Astoria* and *The Rocky Mountains*, which is now invariably reprinted under the title of *Adventures of Captain Bonneville*, are in high demand among collectors of Western material. *The Rocky Mountains* was published in 1837, which for some reason appears to have been a bad period in bookmaking. All the copies I had ever seen up to that time had been foxed, the maps had left marks on the facing pages, and there were numerous other printing flaws. I had concluded that it was just part of any copy of *The Rocky Mountains* to look as if it had come from the press of some woodshed amateur.

Then I got a catalogue from my old friend Louis Cohen, owner of the Argosy Book Store. This catalogue listed a copy of *The Rocky Mountains*, and described it as "mint." In the rare-book trade that means it is practically just as it came out of the bindery. The Argosy Book Store was then about 150 feet from my shop, so I went across the street, without waiting for the light, and inspected their copy of *The Rocky Mountains.* I found it exactly as described and promptly bought it.

It was still lying on my desk when Donald McKay Frost, the great collector of Western Americana, and generally one of the greatest men I have ever known, came into the store. Naturally he picked up the book.

"Everitt, that's almost as good as my copy," he said.

"Mr. Frost," I said, "you have a brief case with you. Put this copy in. If your copy is as good as this, you own two copies. If it isn't, send me a hundred and fifty dollars."

Shortly afterward I got a letter and a package. The letter read: "Dear Everitt: Enclosed is my check for $150. If you can without loss allow me $25 for the enclosed duplicate copy against future purchases, I shall be quite delighted."

Irving's *Sketch Book,* by the way, was originally issued in paper-covered parts. I have never heard of any amount of money that I believe would now bring forth a complete copy. His *Knickerbocker's History of New York,* folding plate and all, is something you can probably reach out your hand and take whenever you have a hundred dollars. But so far only one copy has ever been seen (it once belonged to my friend Luther Livingston of Dodd, Mead and Company) in the original boards, uncut, with paper labels. Money values mean nothing in talking about items like this.

One of my favorite collectors and customers is Bruce Cotten, who lives in Baltimore and spends all his time collecting North Carolina material. His privately printed book, *Housed on the*

Third Floor, is highly unusual in that it represents a collector talking about his own books instead of hiring some cataloguer to do it.

In the book he tells about some of his disappointments. Here is a further setback to add to his list. At the start of World War II a French dealer sent some pamphlets over to the Parke-Bernet Galleries for auctioning. Since his address during the occupation was unknown, the items did not come up for sale until after the war. Among them was one pamphlet on North Carolina, the first and only discovered copy.

Mr. Cotten telephoned to me from Baltimore to find out what the gallery's appraisal was. Their figure was $150.

He told me to go to three hundred. I was nervous about it, called him back, and persuaded him to authorize five hundred.

But unluckily the catalogue description mentioned the shipping of tobacco from North Carolina — an item that probably covered one paragraph in the pamphlet. This was enough, though, and George Arents, the tobacco collector, wanting to fill out the collection he had given to the New York Public Library, sent in an unlimited bid. So I drove him to $500, and at $550 it was his.

Another extremely scarce item that Mr. Cotten mentions in his book is "My earliest Edenton imprint: *Proceedings and Debates of the Convention of North Carolina, Convened at Hillsborough . . . 1787. Edenton, 1789.* This convention, after rejecting the Constitution of the United States, adjourned with much ill-feeling and failed to provide for the publication of its proceedings. A small edition, however, was printed at the private expense of a few gentlemen, and the debates as published were reported by David Robertson of Petersburg, Virginia. Shorthand reporting was novel and unprecedented in North Carolina assemblies at that time, and Mr. Robertson was treated with no consideration, was forbidden the floor of the Convention, and had to be content with 'a very inconvenient seat in the gallery.'"

As for me, the only copy I ever owned was a perfect beauty, in original boards, uncut, for which I paid a scout a hundred dollars.

Soon after I acquired it, William S. Mason, who later gave his collection to Yale, came in and asked the price of the book.

"Seven hundred and fifty dollars," I said.

"All right, send it over to MacDonald and have it bound in full red levant, gilt edges."

"No, thanks. I can't do that to a book like that."

"Why, isn't it my book?"

"No, not yet; it's still mine."

"I'll never buy another book from you," said Mason. And as a matter of fact, he never did.

Among the other charms of Cotten's book is the fact that he gives what I consider to be the best excuse I've ever read for collecting books.

> Book collecting, whether an acquired taste or an acquired nuisance, is in either case acquired. It develops by degrees, and passes through numerous forms and phases, rather curious to look upon.
>
> At first you only want certain sorts and kinds of books and reject innumerable volumes that in after years you are violently seeking. You only by degrees overcome your own prejudices and dislikes and gradually find yourself including and exploring in ever larger fields. Then there is always, and for a long time, a struggle, when you realize that the disease has really gripped you; and numerous determinations are made to stop this thing entirely and not to permit yourself to be classed with those mildly deranged people who collect things.

There are collectors of buttons, tobacco tags, boxes, inkstands, clocks, corks, pins, paperweights, dog collars, and almost everything else on the face of the earth, and as a collector of North Carolina books I have been looked at with shocked amazement by these very same people and made to feel inferior.

Notwithstanding, I have persevered and have insisted that book collecting is superior to all other forms of the disease, though I was shocked and had some misgivings one day upon being introduced to a man in New York who collected only books written by one-eyed men.

Just in case I have whetted your appetite for a copy of *Housed on the Third Floor,* let me say that you won't find one; this is on its way to becoming rarer than any North Carolina item it lists.

Harry Davenport, the actor who followed Frank Bacon in the title part of *Lightning,* married Phyllis Rankin, the most beautiful woman I ever saw. They were both enthusiastic collectors of books about Lincoln.

One day I got a catalogue of a big auction sale in San Francisco, and Mrs. Davenport happened in.

"Oh, my father is sick and I have to go to San Francisco. Wouldn't you like me to attend the sale for you?"

I said that would be fine, and gave her a check for $250 to use as a deposit against what she might buy for me.

About the time of the sale I read that Mrs. Davenport's father, McKee Rankin, had passed on. Soon after, I got a consignment of books from San Francisco, with a bill for several hundred dollars and no mention of any $250 deposit.

Mrs. Davenport arrived soon afterward, very much upset. She said her father had been so ill that she had not been able to attend the sale, but instead had handed my bids and the check to a Mr. Delmas (famous as the lawyer for Harry Thaw). He had attended the sale, but had apparently decided that he needed the check worse than the auctioneer did. The $1500-a-week days of *Lightning* were long past, and Broadway was flat, but Mrs. Davenport said that of course she and Harry would scrape together the money somehow.

I told her not to be foolish and said that the prices at the sale had been so preposterously low that I would not even need to charge the money off to profit and loss.

Some time later I saw an obituary of Delmas the lawyer, which mentioned among other things that he had been an active spiritualist. So, for that matter, had McKee Rankin.

Almost the next day Mrs. Davenport came to the store. "Here's an odd one," she said. "Two days ago I got this letter."

The letter read: "Last night I talked to your father, and he criticized me very severely for being unethical with you. I enclose a bank draft for $250."

The spirits served me better on that occasion than on another, when I was in Buffalo. In the outskirts of the town lived a little character who used to accumulate books from heaven knows where and sell them off to booksellers, usually at a dollar or less apiece. He had a room full of Americana, and I used to look forward to going there as a child does to visiting a toy store.

One evening I picked out an armful of fantastic bargains, and was getting ready to leave when one of the notorious Buffalo blizzards descended on us. When it really snows in Buffalo, nothing moves. My man said I had better stay the night.

By way of passing the evening he and his wife got out two

school slates and produced spirit slate writings from about nine o'clock until midnight. I don't know whether the writing was real, and I don't want to know. I had more hair then than now, and every hair on my head stood upright.

Finally, in desperation, I looked out of the window, noticed that the snow was not much more than thigh deep, and observed casually, "Oh, hell, the storm's all over; I might as well be getting on home."

I footed it for about two and a half miles to the hotel, giving thanks every step of the way.

Beyond the slightest doubt the one towering authority on the Maya civilization was a man named William Gates. My first introduction to him came when a short, seedy-looking individual walked into the store. I was about to hand him fifty cents for a square meal when he asked if I had any books on Central America.

His second remark was, "The only true scientist that ever lived was Madame Blavatsky."

I said, "You must have just come from California."

In spite of this, I found out within a few minutes that he knew more about Central America than any man I had ever met.

I sold him stuff occasionally — with mixed pleasure, because he was always overbought and owed back bills to everybody.

Finally he bought a farm in Virginia, but soon discovered that the only way he could feed his chickens was by selling the library he had spent thirty-five years accumulating.

He sent the library to the American Art Association for cataloguing. They actually printed and distributed an elaborate catalogue, which I skimmed through, and I remember hoping the old man might get ten thousand dollars out of the sale.

Before the day of the sale, however, the authorities at Tulane University in New Orleans, who considered themselves the proper repository for Central American material, became tremendously excited about the collection. Somebody persuaded the president of the United Fruit Company to hand over sixty thousand dollars, with which they bought the collection at private sale; they then hired Dr. Gates as librarian.

Madame Blavatsky, however, proved too much for Tulane before very long, and Dr. Gates had to go back to Virginia.

About this time one of my Explorers' Club friends was a man named Sidney Mackaye, who represented a Toronto insurance company in the West Indies and Central America. On his travels he amused himself by stopping at every crossroads stationery store, looking for local books and pamphlets. He accumulated several thousand very obscure items. Central American publications are almost invariably ill-printed on very poor paper, which seems to attract no one but the insects. Furthermore, printing arrived late in most parts of Central America, so that any local imprint before 1825 is likely to be very scarce indeed, and some as late as 1870 may well be unique.

Finally, on the occasion of giving up his New York apartment, he decided to part with the collection. He asked if I could get him three thousand dollars for it.

In my usual completely naïve way, I thought Tulane University was the proper repository for this collection, so I wrote a letter to the president, whose name my Freudian censor will not let me recall.

He replied, in substance, that all booksellers were knaves and scoundrels and that he wanted no part of any Central American books.

I have quite a collection of these letters, which have always entertained me, and to this one I replied that I could not blame him for his judgment of booksellers, but the fact remained that the Sidney Mackaye collection was available at three thousand dollars. "Furthermore," I added, "if anyone who knows anything about such material will appraise the lot at less than $5000, I will make you a present of it with my compliments."

A few days later a large, sleepy-looking man came in and said, rather as if his mouth were full of potatoes, "Here, here, what's the idea of making me come all the way up to New York on a wild-goose chase? I'm Francis Blom, the librarian from Tulane."

"All right, Blom," I said. "You know and I know the man who knows more about the value of Central American books than all the other people put together."

"I suppose you mean Marshal Saville, at the Museum of the American Indian," he said.

I called up Saville, and he and Blom inspected the Mackaye collection. Saville's appraisal was $5500.

When Blom came back to the store, he telephoned to the president of Tulane, told him what the collection was, and got orders to have it packed and shipped at once. (Blom, incidentally, wrote by far the most popular book on the Mayas.)

The end of the transaction was a draft from New Orleans for three thousand dollars, with a fulsome letter of thanks.

After his brush with Tulane, Dr. Gates went to Baltimore, where with the help of an angel he started the Mayan Society to publish Mayan texts and material. I served as his New York agent. Not one of the publications came anywhere near paying for its printing costs: I remember one Mayan grammar that we simply couldn't give away. By now, of course, his whole series are scarce as hen's teeth, and nearly always worth at least several times their publication price.

The last time I saw Dr. Gates, I went up my steps on 59th Street one rainy morning and found him sitting there without an umbrella.

"Why don't you take care of yourself, Bill?" I asked.

"Oh, I'm all right, Charlie. I'll write your obituary," he said. But two days later his sister, Mrs. H. C. McComas of Baltimore, wired that he had died the day he got back to Baltimore.

The newspapers, which of course had never heard of Gates while he was alive, discovered the morning after he was dead that he had been a great man, and ran column on column of obituary notices.

Shortly his brother-in-law, Dr. McComas, wrote to ask what I would charge to appraise the library that Dr. Gates had reserved from the Tulane sale and accumulated in the intervening years.

I wrote back that I would be glad to do it for my carfare and a steady supply of bourbon.

E. R. Goodridge, the Mexico City bookseller who probably knows most in the world about Mexican and Central American books, was living in Baltimore at the time, and I took him along to lend me a hand.

I knew that the McComases hoped to realize $80,000 out of the library. In one room were several shelves of seventeenth-century beauties that would knock your eyes out. For safety's sake I put Goodridge to collating these, and he discovered that there was not a perfect book among them. After all, a missing map or title page usually means very little to the student, who can find other maps and who knows what the book is anyway. For the collector, and hence for the bookseller, one missing leaf turns any rarity into wastepaper.

In another room was the finest lot of bibliographies of Central America in any private library anywhere. I would have given my right eye for the bibliographies.

At the end of two days' work we sat down to supper with the McComases. I gave them my usual routine: "Do you want the truth, or are you looking for a fairy story?"

They gave the stock reply: "The truth."

"Well, I'm sorry to tell you, but you'll be doing extremely well if you get twelve thousand five hundred for the collection."

That was a bitter pill, but there was nothing I could do about it.

I sat for some weeks and longed for the bibliographies; then Mrs. McComas wrote that a young expert from a Midwestern university, who could plainly have given pointers to Goodridge and me on Central American books, had bought the old books for seventeen thousand dollars.

Next she wrote that Johns Hopkins was going to buy the bibliographies for $2500. I kissed them good-by, prematurely but rightly, as it turned out.

Johns Hopkins couldn't raise the money. I found this out when my dear friend Dick Wormser came home in triumph with the lot. Some Baltimore acquaintance had remarked to him, "Why don't you look at the Gates bibliographies?"

Dick can see as far through a brick wall as the next man, and he had them out of Baltimore that same afternoon by truck.

At least I had the consolation that Dick Wormser got them; if anyone else had, I would have been tearing my few remaining hairs for months.

Some fifteen years ago, while I was at Dauber & Pine's, the head of an auction gallery got a letter from a complete stranger, enclosing a four-page list of books wanted. Most of them were things about as easy to find, on the average, as the *Bay Psalm Book* or a complete set of Caxton's imprints. The auctioneer, apparently thinking himself very witty, referred the man to Dauber & Pine.

His name was Tracy McGregor, and I had never heard of him either. I wrote back that the books he wanted fell in a class of which one bookseller might think himself lucky to see two items in fifty years. But since I noticed that his list referred largely to the American Revolution, I quoted some of the choicer items on our shelves.

He bought them all.

As time went on, I quoted him good Revolutionary material whenever I found it. He was the only customer I ever had who would order 100 per cent of the items quoted.

More surprising, he was the only customer I ever had who would buy more than one copy of the same item.

When I finally met him, a six-footer with a small gray beard, I inquired about this peculiarity of his. He told me (which I already knew) that his great interest was the Revolution; he said there were ten libraries he was interested in, and whenever one of them lacked any Revolutionary item, he would give it to them, regardless of cost. This meant that he would sometimes buy ten copies of the same book.

I was just getting used to my good fortune in having such a customer when Dauber & Pine sent out a miscellaneous catalogue containing seventy-one Stevenson items. McGregor wired for all seventy-one.

The next time I saw him I asked about this; I could not see any connection between the Revolution and Stevenson.

"Well, I was in this library, talking to the librarian, and a kid came in and asked for stuff about Stevenson. They had a set of his works, and one biography, so I thought I might just as well send them along this other stuff."

Of course it is an everyday matter for collectors to leave their collections and money to an institution; but when Tracy McGregor died, he was the only man I ever heard of who left a fund to continue the collections of not one but ten colleges.

Rich and spectacular donors to libraries are very plentiful, as you may have gathered from my stories. The most generous library benefactor I ever knew had, I am sure, no more than ten thousand dollars a year at any time in his life. His name was Daniel Parish, and he certainly contributed more to the collections of the New York Historical Society than any other one man. Of course he got no thanks for it, and was trodden under foot by the librarian; but, nothing daunted, he attended every auction he could hear of, read every catalogue, and hardly ever let a bundle of pamphlets get by him. So far as I know, his sole occupation was buying for the Historical Society at his own expense. The expense ran chiefly to time, because he usually acquired the pamphlets for half a cent or a cent apiece.

The Society showed its gratitude by throwing all of the bundles into the basement, where they rested unopened for decades. My friend Oscar Wegelin is only now, twenty years later, finishing the job of cataloguing.

When my partner Stager discovered (and bought for fifty cents) a copy of Williams's *Narrative of a Tour to the Oregon Territory,* Cincinnati, 1843, which a high authority had called "virtually unknown to scholars," there was a record of only one previous copy, which had been sold for six dollars at the old Stan V. Henkels galleries in Philadelphia.

I went first to Wilberforce Eames. Here was one book that the New York Public Library lacked. Then Mr. Henkels was kind enough to tell me that his sale had been made to Daniel Parish. Mr. Eames spent most of his summer vacation rooting through the bundles in the cellar of the New York Historical Society, and there was Williams.

How many similar rarities fell among Mr. Parish's loot, I do not know. Certainly a good many.

When Mr. Parish died, the executors wrote that they had discovered he owed me $1150. They said the estate was a small one, and it would probably take them two years to settle my account.

I wrote back that it would be a personal pleasure to me to write this amount off my books.

They were old-fashioned New York businessmen, and their reply was the first of a series of checks for $47.92 which arrived like clockwork on the second day of every month until the account was balanced.

2. *The Librarians*

Perhaps it is ungrateful of me, since libraries are by far the biggest buyers of rare Americana, that I have almost no use for librarians; but I doubt that 2 per cent of our librarians even know the function of a library.

Lunching one day with one of the 2 per cent who do, Dr. Randolph G. Adams, I remarked that in fifty years of rare books I hadn't met twenty-five good librarians or twenty-five real collectors.

"I'll pay for the lunch," said my companion, "if you can name a dozen librarians or ten collectors."

I paid for the lunch.

When a man gives an important collection to a public institution, he naturally assumes that the material will be in safekeeping for students forever. Little does he know librarians.

A leading Chicago lawyer, E. L. Cooley, lived a bachelor existence devoid of practically every comfort so he could accumulate a collection of material relating to his home territory in western New York. When he died, he willed the collection to the library in his native town.

Two or three years later, a scout passing through the town was told by the librarian that nobody ever looked at these dusty old books, and she would be very glad to exchange them for some modern fiction that people would read. The scout asked what she valued the collection at, and she said she thought she ought to have a hundred dollars' worth of Faith Baldwin and Warwick Deeping instead of this old collection nobody ever used.

The scout was almost as bad as the librarian because he got out a list pricing the books, many of them rarities, at about 5 per cent of their proper value. I had the luck to get the first copy of his catalogue, and he was unable to fill any subsequent orders from that list.

The librarian of a venerable Eastern university spent twenty-five years assembling a basic collection of Americana. He did it in the days when such material could be found by ordinary vigilance, and at no great expense. Then he died.

His successor, a Scotsman, was interested in nothing but philosophy. He sent for me. I spent three days picking the plums out of this extremely rich pudding. Then I lined up my choices for the new librarian's inspection.

He looked them over and said truculently, "I wouldn't take less than three hundred dollars for these." When I handed him six fifty-dollar bills, he was stunned, because he had expected this price to be in exchanges of philosophy books. I do not dare tell you how many times over that three hundred dollars came home to roost.

It is customary for a librarian to explain to me, and I presume to other booksellers as well, that she has had more experience than I, and therefore knows more about book prices. I learned to accept this gracefully on the occasion when I called at a small Ohio library. A Mr. Hildreth had assembled one of the famous collections of Midwestern Americana and had willed it to this library, where of course the books were immediately deposited in a dark and dusty basement.

When I got there, the librarian went through the routine about her knowledge of book prices. Fortunately I did not bat an eye. She knew that any old book was worth at least ten cents, and so told me that I could have the Hildreth collection for $125, take it or leave it. It was many years ago, but I have always lovingly remembered one item in the collection: a thick-paper copy of the first edition of *The Federalist,* with Rufus Putnam's autograph on the flyleaf. I would happily pay a thousand dollars to see that old friend come back into the store.

I know it is asking for the moon, but I wish all future librarians could spend a year in an old bookstore instead of going to library school. And I wish still more that all present and future librarians would buy, beg, borrow, or steal a copy of Dr. Randolph G. Adams's pamphlet, *Librarians as Enemies of Books.*

* * *

Not all librarians blithely give away priceless collections to the first comer. A big Western librarian, Dr. Frank Root, the author of two volumes of perfectly worthless bibliography of the Midwest, once summoned me to look over his library duplicates. For twenty-five years he had been conscientiously accumulating unbound copies of *Munsey's, McClure's, Cosmopolitan,* and every other useless magazine except the *Police Gazette.*

I found three dusty buildings and several subsidiary attics all bulging with this mass of truck. It took me three days, working with a flashlight, to pick out any stuff that I would even trouble to cart away. I was exhausted by the task, and had really very little idea of what I had finally put together.

Dr. Root said severely to me, "I want four hundred dollars for these." This I thought was cheaper than spending any more time with my flashlight, so I let Dr. Root write out a check, which I signed.

Two days after this stuff got to New York, I had a highly indignant letter from the librarian, vowing I had taken advantage of him.

Meanwhile I had examined the books, and found that I had overpaid him by at least $150. To keep him happy, however, I sent him a signed blank check, with instructions to fill it in with the amount at which I had robbed him.

In reply, he sent back the check, still blank, but said that his real objection was to a middleman's making a profit. He had been studying the various want lists issued by the antiquarian book trade and had discovered that he could have sold at least three of them for three dollars apiece. The six hundred volumes I had so avidly carted away must therefore be worth several times the price I had paid for them. I retorted by mail that if he lived to be ten thousand he might possibly sell as many as one hundred out of the six hundred.

Whatever happened to the rest of the accumulation at his own unfortunate library I have no idea. Certainly the Salvation Army should have been paid to take the stuff away.

During the thirty years William Abbatt of Tarrytown published the *Magazine of History,* he reprinted some two hundred rare items relating to early American history—65 per cent practically unobtainable at any price, 25 per cent obtainable at high prices, the other 10 per cent not scarce. These well-printed pamphlets were issued in very small editions—some say fifty-five copies of each, some say a hundred.

Less than 1 per cent of our American libraries subscribed to this important series.

Six or seven years ago the unsold copies turned up in a bindery. Mr. Abbatt, always being in the red, had left an unpaid bill. There were some two or three thousand pamphlets, and I was glad indeed to pay the binder's bill. In my foolish enthusiasm I decided that one catalogue would sell every remaining copy.

Each item was catalogued correctly—author, title, number of pages, date of the original, and date of reprint; price about a third of Abbatt's original list.

And what happened? Total orders from libraries, $61; one clever dealer bought some for $450; two private buyers bought one of each title.

The type was standing, so I used the same descriptions in three other catalogues. Orders totaled $29.

A sarcastic friend to whom I showed these figures turned around and grinned at me. "What a damn fool you are! Don't you know that librarians buy blurbs, not books?"

For three days I wrote blurbs about books I thought everyone knew.

Net result: telegrams, telephones, special-delivery letters, air-mail letters. In three months not an Abbatt reprint in the store.

I think it is a crime for manuscripts relating to a particular place or state to be anywhere but in the local archives. Some librarians agree with me; some do not.

In trying to get books and manuscripts to libraries where they belong, I find myself succeeding about one time out of five. As I write these words, I hold in my hand a dilapidated folio, broken-backed and loose-leaved, describing in detail the organization, bylaws, organizers, members, reading fees, books on the shelves, a four-page description of the condition of the books, organization of a debating society with signatures of the original members, and many other details of the Dummerston Social Library at Dummerston, Vermont, from 1808 to 1841. There has been some suggestion that this library was the first public or semipublic book collection in Vermont. Many of the records are signed by Hosea Beckley, who wrote one of the fairly early histories of Vermont, published in nearby Brattleboro. Dummerston is now a suburb of Brattleboro, which has shoals of literary and artistic summer residents, memories of Rudyard Kipling (whose house was actually in Dummerston), and, for a town of 10,000, a good and lively public library.

The Dummerston Social Library records were offered to this library on approval for a less than nominal figure. After some nine months of inspection by the librarian, the finder retrieved his material in person.

As I was not the finder, I can gracefully remark that I think you will have to hunt very hard indeed to find a dozen such contemporary records of the founding of an American library.

Next I take the liberty of quoting in full an entry from one of my catalogues:

> Is Idaho Only Interested in Potatoes?
>
> Original Arms of the Territory of Idaho
>
> Lyons, Caleb. Original pencil sketch of the Arms (Seal) of the Territory of Idaho (1866). Lyons, Gov. Caleb. A.L.S. describing the Coat of Arms of Idaho and adding "By the authority in me vested by an Act of the Legislature, passed hereby adopted I have designed above described Coat of Arms for the Territory of Idaho." 1 p. (1866) E. R. Howlett. Certification of adoption and reproduction of seal, April 20, 1866. Three pieces. $350.

When this item appeared in my catalogue, a bookseller was the only one that paid any attention. He wrote: "Everitt, you must be crazy; in Idaho no one has spent $100 for books in the knowledge of man."

But being inexperienced, I wrote the governor of the state, who referred my letter to the historical society. The historian replied, "Our legislature has made no provision to purchase exhibition material." To this I made the obvious reply: "This is not an exhibit—it is in fact a sensational historical document."

No reply to this letter.

As the next move I wrote to the leading Idaho newspaper. The *Pioneer Editor* replied: "Caleb Lyons was known to most Idahoans as a fraud, a sneak, and deep-dyed carpetbagger. . . . I know of no one in Idaho who would give 350 cents for anything belonging to or designed by Caleb Lyons, unless it might be his scalp. Most of the information you refer to is already available in Boise, although not in the original."

My answer: "Am I to understand that Idaho and other state historical societies are only to accumulate documents of honest politicians? If such be the case . . . the many buildings of such societies would be reduced considerably in size. If I know anything about the function of a state historical society, it is to accumulate original material relating to its state."

I quote one paragraph from the editor's reply: "The documents of Caleb Lyons belong in the Idaho state house. I am sure the governor and the historian would welcome them. Perhaps an arrangement might be made whereby the state would go so far as to pay the postal charges in case someone wants to donate the manuscripts."

If I understand this sentence, it means that the manuscripts catalogued are valued less in Idaho than I pay for one Idaho potato in this town.

Thomas W. Streeter, the great collector of Western Americana, finally said, "I don't want the wretched manuscripts, but I like your description." They are now in his library.

I have been greatly flattered when an occasional prominent figure in the rare-book world has chosen me to help put an item where it belongs.

One day Mr. R. W. G. Vail came to me with a shabby bound volume of a newspaper, for which I gave him four hundred dollars with great alacrity. As you see by the following memorandum that Mr. Vail later wrote out for me, this item had been offered to the four institutions where it really belonged. I sent a description to the Wisconsin Historical Society and got $650 almost by return mail. I had first called up Mr. Wall, the director of the New York Historical Society and practically begged him to buy the volume. He told me I had no alternative but to sell it to him at his own price.

Mr. Vail wrote:

When I was working for the Roosevelt Memorial Association — Theodore, of course — I happened to be passing through Canandaigua, New York, while on vacation, and dropped in at an antique shop and asked the proprietor's wife if I might see any old books they might have. Busy with another customer, she waved me to a back room, where I found quite a lot of old books, but none worth buying. As I was about to leave, she said, "There must be an old newspaper in this bureau drawer. The old man picked it up quite a while ago out in the country during one of his trips, and like a darned fool gave $5.00 for it. No one has ever looked at it and I'll bet he's stuck with it. He's always getting excited and paying more for stuff than it's worth."

I looked at the volume, a small folio about three inches thick, saw the publisher's name written inside the cover, noticed the title and date of the first issue, and said, "I kind of like old newspapers, and might be interested in buying this volume if you don't want too much for it."

I tried to keep a poker face, for I realized that it was the publisher's own file of the lost frontier newspaper of New York in the 1790's, the *Whitestown Gazette* — lost, that is, except for three or four stray issues scattered through two or three libraries. Whitestown is now Utica. Here was a practically complete file for several of the earliest years.

She said, "We'll have to wait till the old man gets back — he ought to be here any minute now. It's his book, and he will have to put the price on it."

Just then he came in. "So you are looking at the old newspapers. That's a very fine item. A fellow was looking at it last week and offered me $15 for it. I thought I'd take him up on it, but haven't gotten around to sending it to him yet, so if you want to give me $20 for it, the newspapers are yours."

I glanced at his wife, who looked a bit confused, for she knew that I knew her husband was making up his story as he went along. But I swallowed the yarn, grinning at his wife, and said, "All right, I'll give you your $20 for it." I walked out of the shop with one of the very rarest of New York newspaper files.

Back in New York I took the volume up to my old stamping ground, the New York Public Library, and showed it to Dr. Wilberforce Eames, who was most enthusiastic about it, and very much wanted the library to acquire it, but he referred me to the head of the American History Department.

He liked it too, and then asked the price. When I told him that I wanted $150 for it, the lowest price at which it would ever be offered, he countered with the remark that I had never paid any such price for it, and the library would give me ten per cent more than it had cost me.

So I then took the volume to Mr. A. J. Wall, another old friend, with the price raised to $250. He also turned me down, though he told me several times later that he had made a mistake. My next venture was Dr. J. I. Wyer, state librarian at Albany, but they did not want the precious newspaper at $350, though I later learned that he had not shown my letter to Mr. Joseph Gavit, his authority on early New York newspapers, who would have taken it in a minute. Then I sent a letter to Mr. Pierrepont White of Utica, banker and President of the Oneida County Historical Society. Since his name was White, and Whitestown was Utica, I was rather disgusted when he did not buy the volume out of his own pocket after the society had failed to raise my new price of $450.

That was how the *Whitestown Gazette* passed through my hands.

I once went to Marietta, Ohio, in pursuit of a very important library. My trip was a fizzle, because somebody from Chicago offered five hundred dollars more than I did.

As I was wandering around Marietta, with three hours until train time, I noticed an old, square stone house. I asked a passer-by who lived there.

"Well, an old Civil War general used to, but he died about a year ago."

So I walked up to the door and rang. A very charming old lady opened it.

I handed in my card and said I was scouting around in search of old books.

At this she welcomed me with open arms. "We simply haven't got anything except books." There were books everywhere, even in the bedrooms, and all Americana. Not a set of Charles Reade anywhere in the house. I was nervous at such a good haul as this, so I asked her who her lawyer was. I had long since forgotten and outstayed my train.

"As a matter of fact, he's my son-in-law. Why don't you stay to dinner, and I'll have him over."

He and I soon closed on a good-sized offer. Then I said, "Where is your husband's correspondence with Lincoln and his commission?"

"Over in that old safe there. But I want you to understand that it is not for sale."

"Oh, I understand that perfectly. But it would be a privilege to look at it."

The general had been the Judge Advocate at the Indiana

treason trials early in the Civil War. There were five excellent Lincoln letters and the general's commission.

I asked the general's lady what she intended to do with the papers.

"Well, I think they ought to be preserved in some institution, but I haven't decided where."

"The best institution in this state is the Western Reserve Historical Society," I said. "If I get Mr. Cathcart down here, will you let him have the papers?"

"Oh, that would be splendid. I just haven't known where these things ought to go."

I reserved a room for the night in the very dismal local hotel, and wired to Wallace Cathcart: TRAIN LEAVES CLEVELAND SEVEN P.M. ARRIVES MARIETTA SEVEN A.M. STOP. WANT YOU TO HAVE BREAKFAST WITH ME.

Next morning I went down to the station about forty-five minutes after train time, just at the right moment to welcome Wallace Cathcart. "What did you drag me down here for?" he demanded.

"I told you I wanted you to have breakfast with me," said I.

We had breakfast and then walked for nearly a half mile toward the general's house.

"Do you know who used to live here?" I asked.

"You old scoundrel! I've been ten months trying to get into that house. How did *you* get in?"

"Why, I walked in," I said.

The general's widow gave us a warm welcome, and opened up the safe for Wallace.

After the Lincoln papers and the commission came out, I poked a hand into one of the pigeonholes and hit on seven copies of a pamphlet.

It was entitled, *Constitution and By-Laws of the Golden*

Circle or Sons of Liberty. This organization amounted to an anti-Lincoln conspiracy, and in its day a man found carrying a copy of the pamphlet was quite likely to be shot on the spot.

I muttered out of the corner of my mouth, "Wallace, you only get one of those."

He muttered back, "I do not. I get two."

Being big-hearted, I contented myself with five copies, and struck out for the West.

In Indianapolis, where the general had presided over the treason trials, I fatuously went to see the librarian of the Indiana State Library. When I suggested selling him a pamphlet for fifty dollars, he declared, "I can't see why we should buy this. We already have the reprint from the Government proceedings at the trial."

I gave him my stock reply for librarians: "If you don't see, I'm sure I don't."

Some years ago the librarian at a small western New York college decided that textbooks were more important on his shelves than dusty and neglected oddments concerning America. As soon as I got the good news, I posted out, spent two days at work, and picked myself a large packing case full of reasonably good things, for which I paid $250.

The janitor, of course, was instructed to help me pack up and ship my purchase. Books have to be packed very tight, and I found myself with a hole as big as two fists in the corner of the packing case. I grabbed the first discarded volumes I could lay hands on, juggling them around until they just filled out the space; thickness was what mattered, not contents, and I did not even look at the titles.

Of course these makeweights, being nothing I cared about, were the first things to come out of the case when I unpacked.

One of them bore the fascinating title, *The Christian Advocate,* and I was about to throw it into my capacious wastebasket when the cover fell open, and I noticed some penciled writing: "This is the original first edition of Hayward's *Aboriginal History of Tennessee.*" I had never seen a copy of that either, but I did know it was a very scarce book, so I went straight to Mr. Eames.

It was obscure enough so that even he had to look in his files. "Yes, we've got it," he said, "but our copy lacks the folding plate. May we have your permission to photostat this?"

He paid for that small privilege several times over with the information he had given me, and I catalogued *The Christian Advocate* at $250, basing my calculation on the price of the whole collection.

It was like the Idaho state seal: echo answered.

About this time I was rather struck by the fact that the Library of Congress was buying many books at auction, but none of their business seemed to come my way. I thought it was nearly time to put a stop to this, so down I went to Washington. I called on Dr. Scott, then head of the Acquisition Department, and said I noticed he had not bought anything from me in more than two years, though I was sure some of my catalogues had contained items he lacked. He pressed a button, and the man responsible for checking booksellers' catalogues shambled in. "Do you check Everitt's catalogues?"

"Yes, regularly. He hasn't had anything we want in years."

"How about this?" I said, pulling *The Christian Advocate* from my pocket.

"Oh, I think we have two copies of that," said the acquisition clerk.

"Get them!" observed Dr. Scott.

After enough time to check one catalogue tray and have a change of heart, the clerk returned. "I made a mistake, sir; we haven't got it."

"All right, make out an order to Everitt for this."

I chanced to walk down the corridor with the acquisition clerk, who said in an undertone, "Why should I buy from your catalogues?"

"Look here, old man; don't you think you are a bit late?" I asked.

And I went as fast as wheels would carry me to the Willard Hotel, where James B. Wilbur, the great Vermont collector, was staying.

I told him my tale. "If this ever comes into court, I'll swear up and down that I never heard of it." And in point of fact, I never did.

A few weeks later the book trade journal had a notice that the head acquisition clerk at the Library of Congress was resigning. That's all of that story.

Many, perhaps most, of the mistakes librarians make are corrected in the end when collectors buy up their duplicates and present them to other libraries.

The basement of the Rhode Island Historical Society was absolutely crammed with duplicates, under half an inch of dust and plaster. I said I was going down for a look, but Howard Chapin, the librarian, said no, it was too dirty.

I said I didn't care; I was going. And I went. There were eight and ten and a dozen duplicate copies of rare books, in a shocking state of neglect.

When I was about half through my overhaul, Chapin sent down to say that I was raising too much dust and would have to stop. Then I asked to have the porter bring up my choices.

We agreed on three hundred dollars, which was a fair and square price. Just as I started to pay, Chapin pulled out a bundle from behind his desk. "Want to give me five dollars for these no-good broadsides?"

All I could do was say yes, without looking. The greatest collector of Rhode Island material in the world lived not three blocks away, so my prospect was not very flattering.

Some weeks later I had a phone call from Scott & O'Shaughnessy, the cleverest book auctioneers we have ever had in New York. Walter Scott was undoubtedly the best man I ever saw on the rostrum. They said they wanted ten or fifteen items to fill out their next sale.

There happened to be just eleven broadsides in the bunch from Chapin, so I sent them over, thinking they might bring three or four dollars apiece and pay my train fare.

I sat at the back of the sale, and when the broadsides came up, somebody said, "Two dollars."

Somebody else said, "Three."

Just then Scott turned to me and said solemnly, "Are you bidding on these, Mr. Everitt? I can't quite see you."

I said, "I certainly am," though I had not yet opened my mouth.

With this hint from the auctioneer, I joined in the bidding, and kept pushing until they hit sixty dollars.

Then I noticed that Scott was getting uneasy. He fidgeted and shifted on his stool. So at sixty dollars I fell out.

Mr. Scott took a final, capping bid from the bid sheet and struck off the first broadside.

Practically the same thing happened with each of the other ten.

The lot went, intact, to the collector three blocks from the

Rhode Island Historical Society. Scott told me afterward that he had house bids for $75 each.

Percentages considered, I have been incredibly lucky in some librarians I have known.

Around 1900, in my second or third catalogue, I listed some obscure Canadian pamphlet, eight pages long, for $12.50.

The Canadian National Archives, which had just been put under the care of Dr. Arthur G. Doughty, asked to see the pamphlet on approval, and I sent it.

Soon afterward I heard from Dr. Doughty: "Dear Everitt: I'll be a great many years older before I start paying $12.50 for eight-page pamphlets."

I wrote back: "Dear Dr. Doughty, I'll be a great deal older before I start selling pamphlets by weight."

This was the beginning of a beautiful lifelong friendship. After Dr. Doughty got to know me, he stopped worrying about the bulk of what he bought. His purchases eventually totaled many thousands of dollars.

One morning about ten o'clock I stopped in to call on Dr. Doughty in Ottawa.

He said, "Everitt, I'm delighted to see you, but this is a busy day, and I'm afraid all I can give you is fifteen minutes."

"Oh, I haven't got anything particular on my mind anyway," I said. "I hear Sir Lester Harmsworth has given you a swell collection of Canadiana."

By the time we had finished discussing Sir Lester's gift, it was 4 P.M.; we looked over Harmsworth's pictures, and at long last I started to leave. "Wait a minute," said Dr. Doughty. "I just want to show you that this is the only library in the world where you can really find a map when you want it. You name any American map of any date and any size, and

I'll undertake to have it in front of you, held down by thumb-tacks so that you can really study it, within five minutes of the time you say go."

I called for the first map made by the Samuel Champlain expedition, and it was before me in just over three minutes.

Not long after his map performance, Mrs. Everitt and I found ourselves staying at the Abbotsford Hotel in Russell Square, London, one of a series of English temperance hotels where the only place you could not get a drink was the bar. For our sins, we suddenly became the best friends of an Australian and his wife who attached themselves to us. They persisted in constantly asking us to lunch.

Finally, as the easiest way, we accepted, and they took us to the Royal Colonial Institute. After a lunch of overdone mutton, soggy potatoes, and vegetable marrow (which I don't like much even when it is called squash), our genial host said brightly, "Don't you want to go upstairs and look at the library?"

You probably know how much a bookseller wants to look at a club library, but I decided I preferred the library to Australian conversation, and up we went.

The librarian was supposed to be sitting back of a glass case, which was filled with notes from Thackeray and Tennyson declining invitations to tea and notes from Queen Victoria thanking them for presentation copies of their books.

In one corner of the case was a much less exalted-looking manuscript, and I asked the man behind the case if I could look at it.

He replied, "The librarian isn't here at the moment, and nobody has ever asked to look at anything in this case in the twenty years I've been around. Just a minute, and maybe Sir Charles can help us."

I was not to be put off. I handed him my card and said, "I'd still like to see that manuscript."

He flushed, then disappeared for a moment, and I saw him talking to a short, elderly gentleman in a corner of the library.

This man came over and introduced himself as Sir Charles Lucas, whom I knew as the author of a great series of Colonial histories.

"Well, Mr. Everitt," he said, "what's all the excitement?"

"Sir Charles," I said, "I simply asked to see a manuscript. I know it isn't for sale, but just to make things interesting I'll be glad to give you five thousand dollars for it."

He turned to the assistant librarian and said, "Open that case, please."

The assistant flushed again and said, "We have no key, sir."

"Well, get a hammer or a chisel or something and open it up."

Just then the librarian appeared and he produced a key from somewhere.

When I finally got the manuscript in my hands, I found it was in fact what I had supposed; namely, the journal of Duncan M'Gillivray, the early explorer in the Northwest, with a map that he had drawn from a sketch made by his Indian guide. M'Gillivray had used the Indian's sketch on his way to the Columbia River, since the guide was probably the only one who had been over the route before. There was also a map made by M'Gillivray to plot his discovery.

I asked the librarian, "Has no one ever examined this manuscript?"

"No," he replied.

"Are you sure? What about Dr. Doughty of Ottawa?"

The librarian scratched his head. "Why, now that you mention it, Dr. Doughty was here several years ago and photographed every page of the manuscript."

"I guess I'm not quite so excited about the manuscript," I said, "but thank you very much for letting me see it anyway."

On that trip I was called away from London by a cablegram from my partner, Stager, asking me to look at a library in Ottawa in ten days. The only way I could make it was to go by way of Halifax. In Ottawa I saw the library, offered $4,500 for it, was turned down because the executor had an offer (though not in writing) from an auction gallery for $15,000, and stopped off for a moment to call on Dr. Doughty.

"Here," said Dr. Doughty, handing me a handsomely printed pamphlet, "you might like to have a copy of this new facsimile publication of ours."

I was very glad indeed to have it. It was the first printing of M'Gillivray's journal of his discovery of the Columbus River.

(As for the library I did not buy, there was silence for a couple of years, which brought us to 1930. Then the executor wrote and said he would be glad to accept my offer. I was very glad that my boom-time offer had not been in writing either. A curio dealer finally paid $2,500 for the collection, and I hope he got out whole.)

3. *The Readers*

MORE interesting to me than either collectors or speculators are the readers. It is not much fun selling books to people who can afford to buy them. The real pleasure is in serving the true students, those who are hungry for books that cost more than they can afford.

From long years of friendship the authorities at the Museum of the American Indian (Heye Foundation) know how I feel about readers. Whenever any of the thousands of visitors to the museum ask where they can get books about Indians, they are referred to me. One day the museum sent a postal clerk who wanted to own a copy of Bolton's *Indians of New York City* to me. He sat down at my desk, and I pulled off the shelves a copy of Bolton marked $1.50. He explained that he dared spend only twenty-five cents a week for books. I have always had more fun giving books away than selling them, so I tried to give him this one, but he said indignantly that he was not looking for charity. He firmly put a quarter on the table, and I wrapped the book.

Every Friday for the next five weeks he came in with his twenty-five cents. Then he picked another book, and started buying that the same way.

This went on for some months before he paid me a last visit, and said he would have to stop because his wife had discovered that he was buying books. That story had a sad ending.

Another customer of mine was a shoemaker of West 23rd Street, whose wife was a trifle less vigilant. I kept a bin full of books reserved for the shoemaker, and he was able to sneak two or three volumes a week home unnoticed.

One fine day he drove up — literally — in a horse-drawn hack, marched into the store, and said, "Wrap up all my books!"

"What's happened?"

"My wife just died, and I can buy all the damn books I want."

* * *

For some years I kept framed a letter to me from a Georgia Baptist minister, saying in substance: "Dear Sir: Can you supply any books on circumcision from a Baptist point of view?" I referred him to the American Baptist Publication Society of Philadelphia.

Not long afterward the "list boy" from the New York branch of the Baptist Publication Society came to my store on his rounds. (In those days every bookseller had a boy who trudged around with a list in search of books that had been ordered by customers. The list boy's usual beat was among the publishers, but if an item proved hard to find, he would look in on fellow booksellers.) At the head of the Baptist Society boy's list was an order for a copy of *Fanny Hill.* Probably the Baptist Publication Society was the only bookseller in the country to whom you could have given an order for this title without creating the slightest flutter.

I looked over the list, and, wanting to be helpful to my brethren in the trade, wrote next to *Fanny Hill:* "Try American Sunday School Union."

Somebody at the big wholesale house of Baker & Taylor, entering into the spirit of the thing, added: "Try American Bible Society." To keep the ball rolling, somebody else wrote in: "Try Goodenough & Woglom," who were religious booksellers even more religious than the denominational houses.

I don't know just how long this merry-go-round kept on, but within a couple of days another celebrated theological bookseller telephoned to me and asked if I knew of a book called *Fanny Hill.*

"I've heard of it," I said dryly.

"Well, where can I get a copy?"

"I don't exactly know," I said. "The last man that did know got two years in jail."

Those were the days when Anthony Comstock was making an ever-present nuisance of himself, and I got so bored with trips down to the court of general sessions to testify as a character witness for booksellers charged with selling erotic literature that I thought I would at least have a little fun.

Like most spies, Comstock's stool pigeons might just as well have worn sandwich boards. One of them came into my store on 34th Street one day and said, with a sickly imitation of a leer, "I'm looking for something hot to read."

My face brightened. "Come with me," I said, conspiratorially. I walked him the hundred feet to the back of the store, down the cellar stairs, and eighty feet toward the front. Here I took from a shelf of discards a copy of Hannah Whitall Smith's *Christian Secrets of a Happy Life.*

"I don't think you got me," said the lover of esoterica and curiosa.

"On the contrary," said I, "I got you the moment you started across 34th Street."

When Theodore Schulte first opened his famous bookstore, at 23rd Street and Lexington Avenue, I helped him start, and ran his basement for a while.

One day a very aged Negro clergyman from Georgia came in. "I forgot what book I came in for," he said uncomfortably. "My brethren gave me some money to buy a book, and all I know is that it is a commentary some Baptist wrote on the Bible."

"His name was Adam Clark," I said. "Just a minute." I brought forward the six plump volumes.

"What's this going to cost?"

"Seven and a half," I said.

The clergyman dug some coins out of one pocket, two dollar

bills out of another, then unpinned some more paper money from inside his vest, where it had been safe from robbery. The pile added up to $7.85. "Will the thirty-five cents pay the postage?" he asked.

"Oh, we'll be glad to pay the postage," said I.

I asked him if he had his ticket home, and he said yes. I asked if the thirty-five cents would pay for his food.

"Oh, I don't need to eat till I get back to Georgia," he said, and went out happy.

You probably know about the hunger and thirst of the Donner Party, the travelers who, caught in the Sierra Mountains in winter, finally ate one another.

That hunger and thirst is mild compared to that of a collector lacking one volume to complete his collection. Hunger for books is, in some people, the thing that will break down all inhibitions and hesitations. It is no respecter of person or station.

Thirty years ago I spent an unproductive week of book-hunting in New England. I just couldn't find anything to buy. Two or three booksellers told me that the theological library of Reverend Samuel Hart, at Middletown, Connecticut, was for sale. There was nothing I wanted less than theology, but I was desperate for a few books to pay my expenses. So I went to call on Mr. Bliss, Dr. Hart's executor.

Mr. Bliss showed me some seven thousand volumes of standard theology. It was enough to put any rare-bookseller into a sound stupor. Dr. Hart had been known as the great authority on Bishop Samuel Seabury, the first great Episcopalian bishop of Connecticut. The Hart library, however, seemed to have not a single volume about Seabury.

"What about the Seabury things?" I asked Mr. Bliss.

"I guess that must be the stuff that's piled in the hall," he said, taking me out there.

In stacks on the floor was probably the best collection of Seabury material ever gathered together, as well as a copy of every Episcopalian prayer book ever printed in America. The booksellers who had tipped me off had also let me know that the price on Dr. Hart's collection was three hundred dollars. I said to Mr. Bliss, "I can give you five hundred dollars for the lot."

"I'm sorry," said Mr. Bliss, "but I can't decide tonight, because Mr. Schulte, the theological bookseller, is coming up to look over the collection tomorrow."

I put my watch on the table. "It's eight-thirty now," I said. "Until nine o'clock I'll give you five hundred for the lot. After that, I shan't be interested."

"Isn't that rather a tough way to do business?" he asked.

"Well, I'm not terribly concerned about other booksellers," I said. Mr. Bliss's wife was out of town, and he telephoned to her. Even over the phone, her "Yes, yes, yes!" could be heard across the room.

I handed over my check, and Mr. Bliss asked what I was going to do next.

"Well," I said, "I'll take a few of these pamphlets along to the hotel with me now, and I'll be back at ten tomorrow morning to pick out what else I want."

I packed up two good-sized bundles, consisting of all the prayer books and all the Seabury material, and set off for the hotel. By the time I got there, I decided that it was rather foolish to go back at all, except that it might have hurt Mr. Bliss's feelings. I already had everything of any consequence in my two bundles.

But I went back anyway, and Mr. Bliss introduced me to

Dr. Hart's successor in the Episcopalian pulpit in Middletown.

The new minister was lost in admiration of Dr. Hart's collection, which he told me was the finest theological library in Connecticut. To him its value was not at all diminished by the forty-one volumes I had chosen out of the seven thousand.

"Would you like to buy what's here?" I asked.

"I'd simply love to," he said, "but I can't possibly afford it."

"Could you afford seventy-five dollars?" I asked.

It took me some time to convince him that I was not trying to be funny. Once he got that through his head, he said yes, he could afford seventy-five dollars.

"All right," I said. "Write out a check for seventy-five dollars to Mr. Bliss. I wasn't going to take these books out of the house anyway."

This is rather a long way around to the hunger for books. The telephone in our store on 33rd Street was, for some reason, in a separate room. Besides the telephone we had a table on which we used to put books before we priced or investigated them. The Seabury and prayer-book collections immediately went on the table.

One of our steadiest customers was a clergyman who used to come in every week. He happened to use the phone just after we had laid out the Seabury books, and when he came away, he told me he had a complete set of American prayer books except for a copy of Debrett's *Proposed Prayer Book* of 1789, published in Philadelphia. He had seen a copy by the telephone and wondered if I could sell it to him.

I explained that my copy, too, was part of a complete set, which I could not possibly break up.

The clergyman looked crestfallen, and I thought the subject was closed.

A few days later he used the telephone again. When later

I happened to glance over the Seabury books, I did not see any Debrett.

This was in October. I did not know of anything I could do about it except mourn my shattered set, which, as you can imagine, I did most heartily.

The day before Christmas, the yuletide spirit apparently got to work. I had a mysterious present from an unknown admirer, a parcel mailed in Brooklyn, with my name out of a newspaper advertisement pasted on for a label. As I never saw this particular clergyman again, I was unable to ask him whether he had sent the package. Anyway, the missing Debrett was inside. The collection, thus restored to completeness, eventually went to the William L. Clements Library, Ann Arbor, Michigan.

Some time afterward I decided to give the back room its monthly sweeping. Among the rubbish on the floor was a piece of paper perhaps six by eight inches. Glancing at it, I saw some lines of script in the hand of Dr. Samuel Hart. It read: "This is the only known fragment of original manuscript of the first Proposed American Prayer Book, written by Bishop Samuel Seabury."

Any fool could see that this belonged in the library of the General Theological Seminary, the headquarters of high-church Episcopalianism in this country. I took the paper down to Dr. Denslow, the dean, who told me that a board meeting was just going on, and asked me if I would wait and talk to the members.

The first question the board asked me was whether I would guarantee that this fragment was in Bishop Seabury's handwriting.

"On the contrary," I said, "all I will guarantee is that I don't know. But certainly Dr. Hart is the great authority on

Seabury; his opinion should be worth more than mine."

I had made a price of $250. "How did you arrive at this figure?" they wanted to know.

"It was the first one I happened to think of," I said. "If you give me time to think a little longer, the price may be several times as high."

"Gentlemen," said Mr. Denslow, "I vote we pay Mr. Everitt two hundred and fifty dollars for this before he has time to think any further."

My memories of Bishop Samuel Seabury are, I fear, a little happier than those of his descendant Judge Samuel Seabury. He told me a good many times that he wanted a copy of one of his family genealogies.

Finally a scout came in with a copy, which I bought for forty dollars. Trying to be a good fellow, I sent word to Judge Seabury saying he could have it for fifty dollars.

He came in, looked the book over, and said, "I've wanted this book for forty years, but I think I can wait another forty years before I'll pay fifty dollars for it." And he marched out.

Less than an hour later Michael Walsh of Goodspeed's handed me fifty dollars and departed rejoicing with the genealogies.

The next morning Judge Seabury was on the phone: "You know, I was restless all last night because I didn't buy that genealogy. Will you send it to me?"

"Judge Seabury," I said, "I'm sorry, but I'm afraid you're going to have to wait that forty years for another copy."

PART III
The Trade

1. *The Booksellers*

IF THE rare-book trade seems to you a fabulously profitable calling for a strange breed of adventurous yet profoundly learned beings, I can tell you why.

Every dealer who does not die broke (say one in five hundred) makes occasional big killings. Like me in these pages, he remembers and tells about the jackpots. Averaged out over a business lifetime, the killings melt down to a living wage, sweetened by the adventure of the chase. The adventure is there, no doubt of it.

And the learning is there, too, much of it or little, depending on its possessor. Fundamentally a bookseller or any dealer in antiquities has no capital, no equipment, nothing but his knowledge. A Philistine friend of mine once remarked that the only difference between Poe's *Tamerlane* in the original wrappers and a slightly defective copy of *Poems of Passion*, by Ella Wheeler Wilcox, is in the knowledge of the book-hunter who discovers them.

A bookseller who does not know what he's got has nothing – unless he knows where to find out. (If you read the chapter after this one, you will see that here, too, it isn't what you know, it's whom you know.) I have made money sometimes out of things I knew nothing about; but I used the jujitsu trick of taking the things to customers who did know, and letting the customers sell themselves.

When people talk about business and start proclaiming that you don't need any capital, it is very easy — and usually correct — to suspect them of living on an income. And if Dr. Rosenbach lays out $38,000 for a small piece of paper, it may not seem very helpful for me to say you can go into the autograph business tomorrow with fifty cents.

But you can. If you know enough, you can even stay in business. The only obstacle is the cost of learning. In a pinch you can always find someone — a brother dealer or possibly a customer — to lend you the money for a sure cinch. All that's required of you is to recognize a sure cinch when you see it. You may not have a building as big as the Parke-Bernet Galleries, but neither will you have their payroll to meet.

The old-book business is rather like an iceberg: the shining peak is only a fraction the size of what's under water. The American dealers with mahogany-paneled shops and grilled bookcases containing *Pickwick* in the original parts can probably be counted on your fingers and toes. For every Rosenbach or George D. Smith there have to be a hundred feeders to keep those grilled bookcases full.

Suppose I start at the beginning. Where do old books come from? Where do they go to?

They come from the publishers as new books. Sometimes the publisher purposely makes or pretends to make them rare right then by issuing a limited edition. During the 1920's there were dealers and "collectors" (see *The Mechanical Angel*, by Donald Friede) who simply bought the new limited editions indiscriminately as they were issued and turned them over like stock shares.

Much more likely the new books are not rare enough—the publisher prints too many. When he has sold all he can at the original price, he goes to a "remainder man," a wholesaler who lives on publishers' mistakes. The remainder man probably buys a thousand copies of *History of Corn County, Iowa,* a five-dollar book, for thirty-five cents apiece. He then sends out a catalogue to thousands of drug- and department stores and a few secondhand bookshops, listing *Corn County* at seventy-five cents, along with two or three hundred other flops and ex-successes.

Then one of two things happens. The first is practically nothing: little by little copies of *Corn County* trickle away until the remainder man has four hundred left, which he sells for wastepaper.

The second is that some smart Americana man in Des Moines or Cedar Rapids (who has read the book, but of whom the original publisher has never heard) sends in an order for a hundred copies, and another hundred, and another, until bingo, no more copies of *Corn County* are to be had. The smart Americana man has been sending out catalogues too, but not to department stores and not with a blurb saying, "Was $5, now $1.50." His catalogue goes to librarians and specialist booksellers (not secondhand stores) and Midwestern collectors. It says, "Among the finest of Midwestern local histories. Contains first printing of the pioneer journal of Gabriel Hornblower, a stranded Mormon emigrant. Out of print, but I can still supply clean copies at the original price of $5."

If our man is very smart indeed, he quietly sits on the last ten copies, hoping he will live long enough to get $15 each for them. He may not have to grow so very old at that. The WPA guide to North Dakota is worth that much right now, just because nobody wanted it at the time.

Well, some of the copies of *Corn County* have reached the bookshelves of private citizens in Los Angeles who want a memento of home, and a good many more have landed in bookshops and public or institutional libraries.

The bookshops – barring our Americana friend – soon tire of giving up shelf space to a dingy gray book with no jacket, and *Corn County* goes on the two-bit table. This is one chance for the hypothetical you to start in the rare-book business on limited capital. Supposedly you know that *Corn County* contains a Mormon narrative; you know where to find a copy for twenty-five cents; and you know someone in Salt Lake City who simply has to have every Mormon narrative in print. Percentagewise your profit will be a great deal larger than if you could afford to slug it out with Rosy for a Gutenberg *Bible.*

As for the library copies of *Corn County,* you can get those with a flashlight, a dust cloth, and a copy of *The Case of the Shoplifter's Shoe* as trade goods. For that much in trade you are rightfully entitled to a Howe's *Virginia Historical Collections* as well – published before the Civil War, and hence quite out of date. That there might be anyone fool enough to pay $25 for a copy is not the librarian's lookout; she knows about the real values of books.

The copies belonging to the Angelenos from Iowa also gather dust, and probably don't get back into the book trade until half a generation later, when the daughters-in-law of the deceased call in the junk man to clear out the attic.

Obviously the mahogany-paneled book potentates can't search either Los Angeles attics or two-bit counters. For perhaps thirty years it won't be worth their while having a copy of *Corn County* on the premises anyway. But once it has aged on the shelf, they can pull in their needs through one of the most completely disorganized and smooth-working business structures in existence.

Since the machinery is smooth-working only when you know what button to press, I will take time to describe it.

There is an organization of antiquarian booksellers whose true function is to improve the commercial manners and morals of the members. It plays no great part in the operation of the business.

Next there are a number of magazines, led in America by the weekly *Want List* and *Antiquarian Bookman,* that provide a sort of exchange and stock market. For ten or twenty cents a line you can run a list of books you happen to want.

Theoretically this sends the entire old-book trade scurrying to its shelves, thereafter to deluge you with post cards offering good, bad, and dilapidated copies of *Corn County* at prices from one to twenty dollars. (In case you should ever want to send out a quotation card, remember that it should carry the author's name, the title fully enough to avoid any possible confusion, the edition number if you know it, the place and date of publication, publisher, the condition with note of any appreciable defects, and the price you want for the book. Sometimes the size and number of pages are important.)

Actually the scurrying by the trade will not be so brisk. Books in want-list ads fall into three classes: the rarities, which the boys would rather sell to their own customers; the mildly out-of-the-way, three- to ten-dollar books, for which you will actually get some quotations at prices running from the aforesaid one to twenty bucks; and the common, which are not worth a man's labor to find on the shelves, because he can't ask more than fifty cents for them anyway.

In the middle category you will have some offers and can pick the most advantageous – if the quoters have told you enough about the state of the book to allow a comparison.

At the back of the weekly trade magazines, also, are lists of books for sale. So far as I can tell, these are much more eagerly scanned than the want lists. Every so often you find something you have long wanted, offered by someone who doesn't know or can't get what it's worth. However, the Books for Sale lists are always much shorter than the Books Wanted lists.

Behind the pages of the book-finding organs are a bewildering variety of book traders. Not only are there dealers who specialize in every subject you can think of – I don't mean just medicine or science or literature, but specialists in chess books, in weight-lifting and strong men, in Utopian communities, in doll books, in Government documents, in cigarette cards – but there are men who pursue these specialties in a dozen completely different ways, honest and dishonest.

First in the chain of distribution are the "scouts." They are the footloose book-hunters who actually dig in people's attics, paw over other dealers' ten-cent counters, and put up with the officiousness of librarians. A scout has no store, possibly at most an attic or shed, and in many cases no stock. He is the most conspicuous example of a bookseller with no capital but knowledge.

At first glance you might think he is purely parasitic; but far from it. Except for him, the books he finds in attics and libraries would mostly sleep like the dead. As for his purchases from other booksellers, he is famous for uncovering "sleepers." A sleeper is a fifty-dollar book priced at a dollar.

Most sleepers occur just because no bookman, except Wilberforce Eames (who began life as a bookseller's clerk), can hope to know everything. If I have spent sixty years learning to spot the word "Oregon" in Mexican pamphlets, I won't have had much time left to discover what books on archery command premium prices. Suppose I buy a library on hunting because it has some western *Emigrant's Guides;* I needn't be unhappy when a scout pulls out the archery or the fox hunting at a dollar a volume. I could no doubt go to Ernest Gee myself and get five dollars each, but I am – or should be – too busy figuring out how to realize five hundred apiece on the *Emigrant's Guides.*

If I let the scout live, furthermore, he will come back to me with the Northwest Territory manuscripts he takes off some junk cart. And I needn't be afraid he will go straight to my customer and cut me out, because 98 per cent of the time scouts sell only to booksellers and to each other. Having no capital, the scout can't afford distribution costs: he buys, cheap, whatever he knows a bookseller friend will buy from him. And he expects the bookseller to get at least twice the scout's price for what he buys. Of course there are exceptions. On a thousand-dollar item both the scout and the bookseller may be glad to make a quick hundred bucks for little work. A $25 book leaves little enough margin for anyone even if the scout gets the book free, considering the many days when he sees no book worth five cents.

Some scouts operate through the book-finding magazines entirely, guiding themselves by the books wanted, and periodically cleaning house with a long for-sale list.

Next after the scouts are the mimeograph booksellers. They very often have no shop except the back room at home; they may serve as their own scouts (which I and many others have had the time of our lives doing). Their chief asset is a mailing list of customers, to whom they send out mimeographed lists or catalogues periodically. That kind of business means some specialization — so that one customer will eventually buy more than one book — and it generally means a considerable share of library sales. The mimeograph dealer can afford to quote rather lower prices than a man with high rent or expensively printed catalogues. At the same time, really fancy rarities are not constantly appearing on his horizon. The good, serviceable, mildly uncommon books that libraries want make up a large part of his store.

The catalogue dealer is one step up the social ladder. With the present-day price of printing, any book he catalogues at less than a couple of dollars must be regarded as a loss leader, even if he got it for nothing, as he very probably did, tossed in with some tidbit that he paid good money for. Furthermore, in setting his catalogue prices he must take into account that even a catalogue made in heaven will hardly move more than 40 per cent of the items it lists. Each book sold has to pay for the cataloguing of one and a half books still on hand.

Really good book catalogues are works of art, and sometimes downright bibliographical masterpieces. I have mentioned Ernest Wessen's *Midland Notes*. The old catalogues of Maggs Brothers in London find a ready sale among booksellers as reference books.

What I think of the *average* book catalogue I have already said; for some reason I feel that an ignorant bookseller is more insufferably ignorant than an ignorant grocer. The least he could do is to refrain from putting his ignorance into print.

Many, perhaps most, catalogue dealers have a shop where customers can get waited on, if they wait long enough. A shop and walk-in trade bring a new set of problems. You have to keep a wider variety of books, many at prices that don't really pay for the overhead and handling; you have to deal with a lot of inquiries for the works of Plato in the Modern Library and other perfectly legitimate but financially unrewarding wants. If you keep a store, you tacitly agree to supply what the sidewalk customers ask for. In other words, you have a general bookshop (even though you may not carry new books) rather than a rare-book shop.

I've had both kinds, and both have their rewards. So far as money goes, in recent years mine has all come from a steel cabinet beside my desk where I keep the cream of the crop. The yards and yards of shelving have been filled with stuff that came in through the transom, and I have been lucky when I didn't lose money on it.

Some dealers specialize in subjects; some in methods of operation; and some in customers. The man with half a dozen big learned libraries or well-heeled collectors on his string naturally concentrates on them. His problem (even more than that of any antique dealer) becomes one of supply, not demand. As a result, he will probably charge higher prices, but work on a smaller percentage margin, than a dealer with a more varied trade.

This tendency goes to its logical conclusion in the buying agent. Nearly any bookseller will attend auctions for 10 per cent of the price on your successful bids; some booksellers specialize in the job. Obviously there's no living in it unless the items are big and profitable. Equally obviously there is no risk.

The risk – and hence the mark-up – is smaller all the way through when you know that the Huntington Library lacks some $500 rarity and wants it badly. Just on suspicion you probably couldn't afford to buy the thing at all. As it is, you go $400, and charge $550. The dealer with a general trade can't buck you for things you really want.

I don't need to point out the business advantages you have in that way. But the customer gets advantages, too. He pays somewhat more for what he gets – and he does get it. He is paying you for knowing what his collection still lacks, and for going out and finding it. He also knows that if there's any trouble, you will make good. Presumably, since you are his regular dealer, he is paying you to know enough and take enough care so that there won't be any trouble. I have always maintained that any collector, rich or starving, should pick a dealer he can trust, and trust him. A collector is likely to be quite old before he knows more than a competent bookseller about the books he collects.

Auctions are another form of bookselling that takes various shapes. A hundred years ago American publishers used to sell their standard books at auction to the booksellers. One or two smart operators have also auctioned remainders. Now there are very few auctioneers who hold big sales of important books, with elaborate catalogues and publicity, at which booksellers and the mink-coat public are equally welcome.

In England the book auctions are primarily for the trade, and the public, though not actually excluded, is not cordially invited. For that reason the dishonest "knock-out" system, prevalent in England, has never made much headway here. In this system the booksellers form a ring and set ridiculously low prices on the items they want; different members bid in these items, the other accomplices abstaining, and the whole crew divides the profit.

The big auction galleries almost always sell on commission

for consignors, though I have known rather fat parts of a consignment to get lost temporarily and reappear, ownerless, in some later sale.

Another kind of operation is the small-time book auction gallery that has grown up in the past twenty years. These dealers will handle nearly anything between covers; successful bids of thirty-five and fifty cents are commonplace, and the high spot of a sale may bring $150. The cataloguing, of course, cannot be elaborate, although it has to be passably good because a great share of the bids come in by mail from out-of-town buyers. The small galleries often buy their material outright, on speculation; they perform a commercial rather than a service function.

Every so often somebody – usually an amateur dealer who does not know how to price his books – holds a postal auction, or perhaps he merely runs a books-for-sale ad: BEST OFFER TAKES. I don't know much about these; I've always been too busy trying to buy and sell books without doing somebody else's pricing for him. And you always have an uneasy suspicion that unless the bids are extravagant, the books may sit right where they are, best offer or no.

One last reason why I call the book trade a disorganized and smooth-running machine is that booksellers are apparently always taking in each other's wash, finding a sleeper here, selling it to another dealer, back and forth, as if private customers were the last thing in their minds. But eventually the book reaches the dealer who has the customer.

Now, where do books go? They go from publisher to bookseller to customer to junk man to scout to dealer to dealer to dealer . . . to customer, and sometimes to one of the 2 per cent of libraries where the librarian knows what he's doing.

The process takes time, sure; but rare-bookselling is almost the last remaining trade with the charm of leisure. It isn't a hurried man's calling, any more than it is a lazy man's.

That, roughly, is how the trade operates. As to how a trader should operate, what I consider the very foundation of successful rare-bookselling may seem to you a rather childish attainment. I mean knowing the mere physical appearance of wanted books. With all the reference volumes in the world but without a trained eye and a keen memory, you had better sell coal instead of books.

Even in my old age I can call titles off a bookseller's shelf (unless, of course, they have been rebound) from at least twenty feet away. Between sheer memory and an eye for physical appearance, you can go a long way with almost no other equipment.

One day when I was roaming Fourth Avenue, seeking what I might devour, I saw a pamphlet in the window of a man named Deutschberger. On the plain outside wrapper someone had hand-lettered "Mr. H."

Just a week before, I had been religiously studying, as was my habit, the new catalogue of George D. Smith, perhaps the greatest American book merchant of all time. Fresh in my mind was his full-page description of the first play by Charles Lamb printed in America. Mr. Smith's price was five hundred dollars; Deutschberger's was fifty cents. I hired a barkeep friend to buy the pamphlet for me, lest Deutschberger get excited.

Happenings like this lend a double point to my friend Frank Dobie's words of wisdom: "Luck is being ready for the chance." After four hours of the most astute and intensive dickering I sold *Mr. H.* for $350 to my very close friend Evert J. Wendell, the brother of Barrett Wendell.

I presume the pamphlet was part of the eight carloads of books that Mr. Wendell left to Harvard. When he died, I missed our interminable sessions of haggling more than you would believe. In addition to the drama collection that was his main interest, he had a strange weakness for Laurie Todd, a famous seedsman of early nineteenth-century New York. I bought one of Todd's diaries at an auction for a dollar, penciled $10 on the back of it, and threw it in the bin reserved for Mr. Wendell.

Mr. Wendell came in around nine at night, as he generally did, and I pointed out the Todd diary.

"Bully!" cried Mr. Wendell. "How much?"

"I didn't pay much for it, E. J.," I said, "so you can have it for fifty dollars."

An hour later we had agreed on a price of twenty-five.

"I always wanted to show you you weren't so hot as you thought, E. J.," I said. "Look on the back for my selling price."

"Now what do we do?"

"Now we go to Keen's Chop House, and you buy me fifteen dollars' worth of dinner," I said.

Nobody was ever less mean with money than Mr. Wendell. He cared nothing about prices; he wanted the fun of dickering.

Marshall's portrait of Lincoln is one that you see almost everywhere; most dealers sell it for around ten dollars. Personally I think it is a horrible thing, but I somehow found myself with sixty-two copies. Mr. Wendell saw them on one of my tables, decided to give them away to his friends, and asked how much.

"Oh," I said, "take the lot for fifty dollars."

"C. P.," he said, "that's the first time I ever found anything cheap in your store." And he bought them.

Two or three weeks later I needed a copy to give away

myself, and I phoned Mr. Wendell to ask if he would let me have one back.

It was three days before the engraving reached me from Mr. Wendell; and when I opened the package, I found a bill from Fridenberg, the print-seller, for ten dollars. Mr. Wendell's collection had long since overflowed from his house into a warehouse, and he was quite unable to find one of his own sixty-two copies. From what I know of college libraries, the sixty-two are probably still tied up in brown paper in the basement of Harvard University.

One of the pleasantest and almost unvarying routines in the rare-book world is that by which you go into a store, ask the bookseller if he has anything new, to which he usually replies no, sit down, and begin passing the time of day. Meanwhile, however, your eyes are wandering around the shelves. (Memory again.)

In nearly every store you will see a set of *Appleton's Encyclopedia of American Biography,* bound in red cloth, in six volumes. It is worth about three dollars a set. But if you can count as high as seven, and there is a seventh volume, the value of the set is multiplied by about ten.

Again, take what is still unquestionably the best book on early American manufacturing: J. Leander Bishop's *History of American Manufactures.* In my younger days I used to buy the two-volume set for about fifty cents. Nowadays I am lucky if I can occasionally find a set to sell for twelve dollars. But here is the joker. Volumes one and two were issued successively; then the Civil War intervened; finally a volume three was published. Actually the extra material in volume three does not offer very much extra information, but it raises the price of the set to thirty or forty dollars.

It often happened when volumes of a set were published one after another that the subscribers would dwindle away, and the last volume would be printed in a much smaller edition than the early ones.

A very striking example is the bound volumes of *Niles' Weekly Register*, which began publication in 1811. It is an extremely important historical source; I might be tempted to call it the *Time* magazine of its day, except that it was written in English. The complete file runs to seventy-three volumes, of which the first forty or fifty are reasonably common.

The last fifteen volumes, which were printed in a larger format than the previous ones, are practically impossible to find at any price. These volumes contain many narratives of Western travel that have never been reprinted in books or any other form. You will find a good many of them listed in the Wagner-Camp bibliography, *The Plains and the Rockies.* And remember, the larger physical size is the tip-off.

In the *Antiquarian Bookman* of June 3, 1950, Jacob Blanck, one of our really great living bibliographers, quotes the following about book collectors from the *Indiana History Bulletin:*

> The state of Indiana owes a good deal to its collectors. These are the men and women who gather up written records, artifacts, pictures, and museum objects and preserve them against loss, dispersal or neglect. . . . By putting a monetary value on the oldest and scarcest printed and written materials that were produced here, they have made other people more careful about what they throw away or neglect. Drawn from attics, basements, barns and bookcases, are pamphlets, books, broad-

sides, maps, letters, diaries, ledgers, deeds, etc., that help reveal the story of early Indiana.

Those words, in my opinion, apply almost entirely to booksellers rather than book collectors, and I will bet that if the Indiana Historical Society checked over its acquisitions, it would find that at least 75 per cent had come from booksellers such as Clark and Smith of Cincinnati, Ernest Wessen, Wright Howes, and their fellows. Rescuing from garrets and barns is almost never done by collectors; booksellers do it.

Here is a letter I had from Wessen some years ago:

> Mrs. Wessen and I were returning from a visit to the folks in Maine, and dropped in at a scout's home near Mansfield. He greeted me with the query as to what I would pay for the original account books of a grist mill, run in Belmont County, Ohio, in the year 1747. A hell of a question, for there was no grist mill in Ohio at that time . . . no Belmont County . . . no Ohio, if you please. He brought forth a Hell of a leatherbound tome, which seemed to indicate that it was the records of a mill somewhere in England. I afterwards found out . . . Plymouth, England.
>
> I didn't want it, but wanted to keep him sweet so I bought it for the seemingly atrocious price of $40.00. Stuck between its leaves that night I found a letter from Henry Knox appointing one Josiah Fox as Chief Clerk of the Navy, but . . . giving Fox to understand that he would have charge of the design of the frigates about to be built . . . 1794. Then were found a few random sketches of parts of naval vessels.
>
> The next morning . . . five o'clock to you, you New York stay-abed, I was at the scout's house, but could obtain no information from him. "Yes, at a Hell of a price,"

he said, there was a lot of material to be obtained. That night he showed up at my house, and got us out of bed around midnight with two large cartons filled with more papers "about the mill." About the third paper I opened happened to be a letter from Paul Revere bidding on the "copperwork" on the frigate to be built at Boston . . . "OLD IRONSIDES." We paid our man off, and Mrs. Wessen and I sat up all night going through the stuff. All night? Until three P.M. the next afternoon with an occasional bottle of beer and a sandwich served by our then tot Ruth.

Here beyond all doubt were, in small part, the papers pertaining to the construction of the first U.S. Navy . . . authorized in 1794 . . . and though at that time I knew not one damned thing about the history of that first Navy, I had to go to work.

But . . . back to the scout . . . The next day I was again at his door stirring him into action. He hadn't the slightest idea as to what had turned up, but drove off and came in a few hours later with another couple of cartons . . . and there he made his mistake. For here again was but a tantalizing fragment of a whole which I knew must exist somewhere in Ohio.

However the address labels on these second-hand cartons all clicked. That evening I went to him, and said: "Either you go down and buy the entire lot tomorrow, or I shall." "How to Hell do you know where they are?" he asked. I took a long shot and named the addresses on the labels of those cartons . . . and clicked!

That afternoon I went to the bank and got all the cash the Wessens possessed. The next morning at 6 A.M. I was at my man's house; picked him up, and we went to Belmont County . . . where I met a delightful old Quakeress Anna Fox, the grand-daughter of Josiah . . .

and the old lady remembered him vividly. Got some young relatives to come in and attest to her qualifications to transact business . . . for she was in her nineties. Then we started to comb the house. Bought all loose papers, and, as we were leaving the attic I saw rolls of paper . . . "Wallpaper remnants," she assured me, but I was seeing everything. They turned out to be the original draughts of not only the CONSTITUTION and her sister ships, but the CONSTELLATION, and Fox's famous WASP and HORNET, and his equally infamous CHESAPEAKE, in which (at the demand of the Navy Department) he had gone back to the English style of construction.

Now for research . . . I found that a man who had never gone to sea . . . a man who in twenty years had never built an outstanding ship . . . Joshua Humphreys of Philadelphia . . . was accredited with designing the notable CONSTITUTION and CONSTELLATION . . . and despite great activity then and there dropping out of sight, while my man Fox went ahead to design the truly beautiful WASP and HORNET as well as other ships.

You don't handle old books very long before you become conscious of scouts, the usually impecunious middle-middlemen who pull the books out of attics and sell them to booksellers. It seems like an almost foolproof business because there is no overhead and seldom much investment. Nevertheless, scouts, like horseplayers, usually die broke. Their trouble is that instead of taking a profit and being satisfied, they constitute themselves a sort of walking auction. They go to one bookseller, get an offer of five dollars for a book, and then go to another with a request for six.

One of the worst offenders I have known was a former

letter carrier who built up quite a business by always asking, as he left the morning mail, whether there were any old books in the house.

This man was constantly using my offers to start the bidding. I was also annoyed with him because he once came to me with what looked like a rather important lot of Andrew Jackson letters, for which he wanted three hundred dollars. When I looked them over, they were not nearly so important as they should have been. I asked, "Are you sure you haven't got any more of these?"

"No, that's all."

I found he was telling the literal truth when I went to a friend's shop and discovered a hundred really important Jackson letters addressed to the same person as those I had. My friend had picked out the good ones first, leaving the mailman only the froth for me.

The reason why scouts go broke because of their peccadilloes is that eventually such behavior almost always gives the victims a chance to get even. I had my chance when my sharpshooter friend rushed in with a like-new copy of Beck's *Gazetteer of Illinois*, the first statistical summary of the young state.

"Can I use your *American Book Prices Current*?" he said.

Willing to save him a trip to the public library, I said, "Help yourself."

He thumbed through it industriously, then emerged with shining face. "The last copy sold in here brought thirty dollars," he announced. "Will you give me twenty for this?"

It happened that the previous week I had been at a sale where a copy not as nice as this one had brought $350, so I said quietly, "Yes, I'll be glad to."

Not long afterward the sharpshooter was in again, not so

shining-faced this time. "Did you know that a copy of Beck's *Illinois Gazetteer* had just sold for three hundred and fifty?" he demanded.

"Sure I knew it," I said, "and, furthermore, the copy I got from you I sold for four hundred and fifty. I've put up with you for ten years, and I suggest that this close our dealings."

Some scouts don't chisel and don't go broke. One scout named Barrett came into my store on 34th Street. "I've always done all my business with libraries," he announced. "I've never sold a book to a bookseller. Now I'm looking to see if I can find an honest one."

"That's asking too much, Barrett," I said, "but you may find me 50 per cent honest, which is way above the average."

He kept his good stuff – and good is a mild name for it – in a furnished room in Harlem. With people like him I would rather work backward from the answer in pricing books. As I laid down each volume, I would say, "I can get so much for this." Then we added up the figures. "Now, are you willing to let these go for half the retail price?" Barrett said he would be delighted, and for twenty years I was the only bookseller he ever dealt with.

When he reached the age of eighty, he acknowledged to me that he had five hundred dollars in the bank for each year of his age, and he thought that was altogether too much for a man with no family. So he stopped scouting for books.

Considering that scouts really have nothing whatever to live on but their knowledge, they slip up rather often. One slightly shifty-looking character whose name I never did learn used to bring me standard books at attractive prices for a number of years. Finally he arrived with a lot that he sold to me, and then pulled out of his pocket a copy of William

Fleming's *Indian Captivity* in German, printed at Germantown, Pennsylvania, in 1756. "I won't sell you this until I've investigated," he said cautiously.

Perhaps I am being unkind to his knowledge. But how the hell could he investigate a book of which no copy had ever been sold?

I wasn't going to break my heart over this, and anyway within a couple of days I was carried off to the French Hospital. Here I was roused from my bed of pain by a phone call from Harry Alpern, my man Friday. "That guy is here again with his Fleming," he said, "and he wants twenty bucks for it."

"Why the hell don't you give it to him and stop bothering me?" I replied sweetly.

Or if I was not sweet, I should have been because the Fleming paid for my entire stay at the hospital.

Here, incidentally, is an object lesson to show that rare-book prices do not always rise constantly until they reach the stratosphere. I have long thought that, with two possible exceptions, Indian captivities were deadly dull reading, and a pure waste of paper to print. Apparently the collecting public is coming around to my view, because later at auction the German Fleming brought less than a third of what William H. Duncan had paid me for it.

Nevertheless I have a pleasant memory connected with another batch of Indian captivities. A woman came into the store one day with eleven of them, all the seventeenth- and eighteenth-century New England rarities.

She asked rather stiffly, "What will you give for these?"

"Don't go so fast," I said. "Tell me the story about them."

It developed that she had just bought an old house and had found these pamphlets under the eaves in the attic. She decided that she could use a new hat, so she took the lot to some bookseller on Cornhill in Boston. He offered five dollars, but she had her heart set on a ten-dollar hat.

She next went to Washington Street, where an offer of fifty dollars scared her. Then she went to the dealer whom she should have called on in the first place, and got an offer of five hundred dollars.

This really did scare her, so she went first to the Boston Public Library, then to the New York Public. They sent her on to me.

I mentally priced the eleven pamphlets and struck a total. "I can get $1250 for these within a very short time," I said. "How much are you going to let me make for being honest and telling you the truth?"

She said $750 would do her very nicely. As she was putting away my check, she said she could probably get several ten-dollar hats now

Every time a group of booksellers gets together and starts telling stories, somebody chirps, "It can't happen now."

This makes me wild. You may not be able to buy a *Bay Psalm Book* at auction for fifteen shillings the way Henry Stevens did, but even now some old family with connections among the great of past centuries has a fit of housecleaning at least once every year.

Not more than ten years ago I was on Federal grand jury duty. During the lunch hour I wandered down Vesey Street and stopped at a junk shop. Blowing around the floor were some old documents. I noticed one dated San Francisco, 1846, so I started seriously assembling more. I gathered up 181 papers, and asked the proprietor how much.

He was a damn robber, or more likely thought I was, so

instead of admitting that he would take a dollar, he said, "Thirty dollars."

I grinned and handed him $30.

I catalogued the lot of documents very elaborately at $1000. There were items like the six-month struggle to raise $600 for a schoolhouse, and the contract with a schoolmam for $600 a year, unless they could not raise that much, in which case she was to take whatever they had.

The catalogue was simply swallowed up; not a peep about the San Francisco documents. So I catalogued them again, at the same price, this time with a headline: IS THE WHOLE STATE OF CALIFORNIA BROKE?

This finally brought a San Francisco lawyer to the store. He asked if the documents were as good as I had painted them. I said they were a damn sight better.

"Well, send them to Bolton, the state librarian. If he likes them, I'll send you a thousand dollars."

Within a few days I had his check, and a letter from Bolton: "How did these things get to Vesey Street? They belonged to our first San Francisco newspaper editor, and he was run out of here for being a Mormon, and died in South Carolina."

I don't know how the papers got to Vesey Street; I do know that it keeps happening all the time.

During the scrap drive, around 1942 or so, a junk man came into my shop with a carton of old papers someone had given him to cart away. I glanced at them, and surprised him very much by giving him twenty-five dollars.

The papers were diaries and other records of John Pintard. Pintard was a promoter and liver-by-his-wits who flourished in the late eighteenth century, spending his time alternately in jail and contributing lavishly to worthy causes. He was one of the chief founders of the New York Historical Society and the (Episcopal) General Theological Seminary. The New York Historical Society published all of Pintard's papers they could find some fifteen or twenty years ago, in four stout volumes.

These papers were ones they had *not* found, including, as I say, two diaries.

I called up Miss Dorothy Barck, the librarian of the New York Historical Society. "If you want to see the Pintard papers you're missing, you'd better get over here."

"Give me ten minutes."

Each time she picked up a paper, she exclaimed, "This one I've got to have!" There were none left over. Finally she said, "How much?"

"Seven hundred and fifty dollars, seeing it's you."

"We'll take them, but we'll have to hold a meeting." So I sent them over.

Some days later she called up. "It's all right; send us a bill for seven hundred and fifty. But I don't mind telling you that Mr. Wall thought the price was outrageous."

I've been sorry ever since I didn't charge him $2500.

Just a few weeks ago I called on my friend and neighbor Carol Cox, the East 59th Street bookseller, who handed me three or four old deeds. Deeds are poison to booksellers, partly because most of them are of no intrinsic interest and partly because there is almost always an original filed with some county clerk. These particular papers were dated 1797, and all I could make out by inspection was that they referred to some large tract in western New York. There was a large water-color map showing the terrain. I also noticed the signature of Alexander Hamilton on the outside.

The papers meant little to me or Cox, but I knew that R. W. G. Vail of the New York Historical Society (Mr. Wall's successor) had western New York history at his fingertips, so I took a taxi over to show him the deeds.

Dr. Beekman, the president of the Society, was there, and he explained that the Society had no money. This is a permanent trouble of every library I have ever known, so I went right ahead and laid the deed on Vail's desk.

He said to Dr. Beekman, "I think this is a document we have to have; we'll take it up at the next meeting."

I picked a price out of the air, and then asked Mr. Vail what he had bought.

He wrote me the following note about it:

> This was the corrected and final deed for the so-called Chassanis Purchase of 200,000 acres in Saint Lawrence and Franklin Counties in 1797. This is the original deed for one of the great land purchases of the late 18th century in New York State. The land was bought for the settlement of refugees from the French Court at the time of the French Revolution. Many of these unfortunate people who had never worked with their hands in their lives arrived on the purchase in the dead of winter, with storm and snow and the thermometer below zero, to live in log huts under primitive frontier conditions. Needless to say, the original plan of the purchase was a failure but the land was later settled and cultivated by hardier stock more familiar with farming in a bleak climate.

There are almost no printed sources concerning this purchase. Mr. Vail told me that the Massachusetts Historical Society had the diary of one of the settlers, and that is almost all the material that exists.

* * *

For some obscure reason, and despite everything I believe to the contrary, the best buys I have ever made were the things I knew nothing at all about.

An old Austrian called me up from Morningside Heights. He said he had been in Mexico with the Emperor Maximilian and that he had twenty-two hundred volumes in various languages relating to him.

I went up and looked them over. I asked him what he wanted for them, and he made the customary reply, namely, that he had been offered $2500.

I took my hat and bade him a cordial good day.

The next morning he telephoned to ask what price I had in mind. For some reason or no reason, I said, "Three hundred dollars."

"Come and get them."

I, like the usual librarian, put the collection down in my huge cellar on 34th Street.

A member of the New York Public Library staff, Dr. Victor Hugo Paltsits, one of this country's most learned librarians, was washing his hands in my downstairs washroom. When he came up, he asked what that junk was downstairs. I said I didn't know.

He asked what I wanted for it.

I said three thousand dollars.

He asked how I arrived at this figure.

I said because I had paid three hundred.

Dr. Paltsits said, "All right, I'll buy them, if you'll bill them at so much per volume, and let me return any items that we already have."

As I was packing the books — and thus really discovering for the first time what they were — I noticed several items that struck me in my ignorance as quite valuable, such as a complete three-volume file of the daily newspaper that was printed for the Austrian monarch during his unhappy reign in Mexico. But, knowing the New York Public Library's unrivaled collections, I was sure that all the real rarities would duplicate what the library already held.

When I went in to settle accounts with the library treasurer, he said, "Everitt, this is preposterous. At this per-copy rate we are supposed to be paying you eighteen hundred, and every single rarity in the lot is a duplicate. What are you going to do about it?"

"I'm going to collect eighteen hundred and my duplicates," I said.

The treasurer stepped into the next room and returned with a check that had obviously been made out some hours before.

You never know what you have until after you get rid of it. My old friend Harry Stone once raided a famous West Side mansion in New York and laid his claws on a great many rarities. One of them was Captain Bligh's own manuscript of the mutiny on the *Bounty.* He sold it to me for fifty dollars.

I piously wrote to the British Museum, saying that, seeing it was them, I would let them have this for a hundred and fifty pounds.

About two months later they replied that they had no money. (After all, they had the printed book!)

Another dealer friend, John Loomis of Lowdermilk's, Washington, offered me five hundred dollars, and my enthusiasm had flagged enough so that I took it.

Shortly afterward an Australian librarian to whom I told my story said, "Well, I don't know anything about it, but if it's the real thing, I wouldn't mind giving five thousand quid for it."

John had sold it by then.

America has never had a really great bookstore. For a long time the owners of Leary, Stuart & Company in Philadelphia tried hard to put their store into that class. Percy Wilkins, the manager, had a wider general knowledge of old books than anyone in the country except Sam Dauber; and while Wilkins was running the store, it was the most famous old-book place in America. Now it is less than a shadow.

One of the last times I saw Wilkins, I poked around downstairs without finding anything; then I went up to see him.

"Did you notice that folio on the floor downstairs?" he asked.

"No," I said.

"Well, I think you'd better have a look at it."

So we went downstairs. The folio was the well-known album of Catherwood's illustrations for John L. Stephens's *Central American Travels.* In those days it was a good, standard twenty-five dollar item. The peculiarity of this one, however, was that it had been very beautifully hand-colored. It was marked $40, which meant $36 net to me, and I hastily paid up. Afterward I discovered a note somewhere, saying that Catherwood himself had hand-colored ten copies of the album.

At any rate, I was just about to leave Leary's, feeling I had done a good day's work, when Warner, the manager of the Americana department, put a hand on my sleeve.

"I've just had some rotten luck with a rare book," he said. "Here's a copy of Jefferson's *Notes on Virginia,* but it hasn't any title page." I supposed all booksellers knew that this volume, issued in Paris, had never had any title page, and I thought Warner was kidding me. I paid no further attention, and started to leave.

"Here, will you take this cripple for two dollars?" he called after me. I accommodated him, adding $448 to my day's clear profits.

Percy Wilkins was not in on that transaction. I am reminded of another Percy, my friend Percy Loring, beloved of a generation of the publishing trade, who was once poking around on the fifty-cent stand of a New England bookstore, where he found a rather nice first edition of *Moby Dick.* Percy had heard of about three old books, and that happened to be one of them, so he invested four bits.

This particular store was constantly advertising for a first edition of *Moby Dick,* so Percy waited two or three days, until he had covered the rest of the trade in the town on his selling trip, and then marched up to the proprietor of the store. "I see you are looking for a first edition of *Moby Dick,*" he said.

"Yes, I am. How much do you want for this one?"

"Three hundred and fifty dollars," Percy said.

After a considerable amount of Yankee trading, Percy realized that the bookseller could not afford to pay more than $300, and since the man was an old friend, he let him have the book.

I feel entitled to say that we have no really great bookstore in America, because I have known three in Great Britain: Francis Edwards's in London, Basil Blackwell's in Oxford, and James Thin's in Edinburgh.

The first time I went abroad Lathrop Harper wrote to warn Edwards of my coming visit.

I was welcomed by a delightful little man about five feet four, who said, "When you get through here, will you do me the honor to take lunch with me?" He then introduced me to all his department managers, telling each one, "This is Mr. Everitt, on his first trip here. Mr. Harper tells me he knows a good deal about Americana. I want you to make any price concession you possibly can if he finds something that interests him."

Nearly the first thing I laid my hand on was the undated first edition of Herndon's *Life of Lincoln,* which was priced ten shillings. This put my mind at rest about prices. I did discover that the various volumes of early American travels, in accordance with what I found later to be the prevailing British practice, were marked somewhat higher than was our habit in America. In those days not even Edwards himself had had any opportunity to become familiar with Western Americana. The trade overpriced the early travels, from our point of view, because their only contact was with American tourists in London, who felt sure they must be getting a bargain from some ignorant Englishman, and readily paid whatever price was marked.

After I had worked for three hours with Mr. Love of the Americana department, Mr. Edwards took me to lunch at his club. He was a delightful companion, and talked practically every moment; books were not mentioned once. What really interested the greatest bookseller in London was prize fighting.

You may be surprised at my calling Francis Edwards the greatest bookseller in London. There are, as a matter of fact, half a dozen shops with a more valuable stock, and very astute merchants too; but they are all more or less specialized. At Edwards's you can get anything.

I am almost tempted to relent and include Maggs Brothers, because after Mr. Ernest Maggs took me out to lunch and offered me unlimited credit (which I was densely foolish enough not to use), he asked what I was going to do next.

"I've never really looked at a guide to London," I said.

"Oh, fine, I'll send one over. Do come in again."

And within a few minutes a special messenger arrived at my hotel with a guide to London, billed at one shilling less 10 per cent.

The next great British bookstore I saw was James Thin's in Edinburgh. The place is a veritable warren with not thousands but hundreds of thousands of volumes, new and old, all neatly classified.

Or almost all. On a later visit when Sam Dauber and I had been combing the place, Sam went downstairs to wash his hands. He came back up, saying, "There's a whole room down there that we never discovered."

I went down with him. The main thing that attracted us was seventeen folio volumes in red morocco, simply marked, "Maps."

Blowing and brushing off the dust of decades, I pulled out one volume. From it I deduced that somebody had spent a lifetime buying atlases from the sixteenth century on, and had then torn them apart and reassembled the maps to form consecutive volumes on various continents and localities.

We went up to Mr. Thin and said, "What are those old maps downstairs?"

"I haven't the slightest idea," said Thin. "Let me look at my records."

Finally he reported: "I gave fifty pounds for those, twenty-one years ago. As far as I can discover nobody has ever looked at them or touched them since. Would you like to give me seventy-five pounds for them?"

When I unpacked them in New York, Albert Johnston came in and pounced upon them.

I sold them to him, or at least I had his check, and the books disappeared from my store. Afterwards Mr. Johnston could never remember having them. All I know is that I wish I could find them and buy them back for what he paid me.

A few blocks from James Thin's is the shop of John Grant, in George Street. Grant deals primarily in remainders and reprints, but he has a few thousand old books, which seem to come in through the transom of practically all bookstores in spite of the best efforts to keep them out. On one trip, when I was chaperoning my friend Ernest Dawson's Glen, who was abroad for the first time to buy books, we poked around in Grant's for hours.

There was one set of bound pamphlet volumes marked *Civil War*, which I had seen at least a dozen times. I had flashed them without discovering anything whatever to make them worth the nine guineas I found marked inside one of the covers. But Glen was buying a lot of stuff – his father's principle was, "I don't know anything about books; I'll buy any book that looks cheap to me" – and I thought I might as well fill in the time by really looking through the pamphlet volumes. My bored persistence revealed what previous quick glances had not, namely, a copy of Scripps's *Life of Lincoln*, printed in Chicago. The peculiarity of this is that Scripps's Lincoln printed by the *New York Tribune* is a fairly common pamphlet, and was long regarded as the first campaign biography of Lincoln. Then somebody discovered that there had been a Chicago edition a few months before the *Tribune* one. Now the New York edition may be worth $15, and the Chicago edition, $250.

I had just finished going through the volumes in an unavailing search for any further hidden plums when Aiken, the manager of the store, came by.

"Here, Everitt," he said, "why don't you buy these Civil War pamphlets?"

"I don't want to buy them," I said. "I see you've got them marked nine guineas. I'll give you five for one pamphlet."

"Which one?" Aiken asked.

"I'll tell you that after you've said yes or no," I retorted.

Aiken called out to Mr. Grant, "Mr. Everitt wants to give us five pounds for one of these pamphlets, but he won't say which one."

"Neither would I, under the circumstances," said Grant. "Let him have it."

At long last, as I was paying up, Glen announced that he was through. He had in his hand a folio that he thought I might possibly use. It was marked seven shillings, and contained seventy-one newspapers. Some screwball had formed the eccentric notion of collecting English and Irish newspapers that announced the outbreak of the American Revolution.

"How about this?" I asked Aiken.

"Oh, you've spent quite a lot of money, take it along," he replied.

"No, I want to buy it. How much?"

"Well, give me six shillings, if you must."

This far my conscience compelled me to go, because I suspected — correctly — that I could find some foolish collector of Revolutionary material who would pay me ten dollars per newspaper.

I have no very exciting stories to tell about Basil Blackwell, but he probably does not mind, since I read in the *New York Times* the other day that he had just paid the largest income tax of any retail bookseller in Britain.

One of the great specialist booksellers in London is a firm whose name I will not mention because I haven't the slightest idea whether the following rumor about their establishment in London is true. According to the rumor, a butler from a neighboring great estate marched in one day and said reproachfully to the proprietor, "You didn't keep your appointment to come and look at the master's library."

Our man, quick-witted as always, said, "Oh, I'm terribly sorry — was it today? I made sure it was tomorrow. I'll go straight along."

The rumor has it that he paid five hundred pounds for the library, and eventually took a hundred thousand pounds out of it.

When Mr. and Mrs. E. Joseph of Charing Cross Road died, I lost two of my best friends. Old Jo, starting out as a "barrel man," had become an outstanding bookseller, with one of the best retail locations in London.

The south side of his store was, and is, a large brick wall with shelves open to the public. When clerks are not watching, passing dogs frequently use the lowest shelf for practical purposes.

Not to digress, I think more than 50 per cent of all the sermons I have ever heard were written with the help of what clergymen call "homiletic aids." (In school we called such things "ponies.") Among the most famous aids is a set of twenty-one large volumes known as "Simeons" — Simeon's *Skeletons of Sermons.* For many weeks a set of those skeletons was on old Jo's lower shelf. Some weeks after it disappeared, I was gabbing with old Jo when a country clergyman marched in.

He said he was now the owner of Mr. Simeon's sketches, but when he put the set in his library, he began to notice a terrible odor.

Said old Jo, without a smile, "My dear sir, did you not know that you were buying a set of dogmatic theology?"

Some rare-book cataloguers are almost as fond of describing their treasures as "unique" as they are of saying, "Printed in a limited edition of only 150 copies, of which this is Number 76." My reverence for these statements has diminished somewhat with the years. Once, about the time when I was entering the book business, some learned printer in Edinburgh reprinted a limited edition of an actually unique Indian primer. Only fifty copies were printed. It said so right on the back of the title page. Accordingly, the reprints should have been nearly as hard to come by as the original. Some years later when I was going abroad, Marshal Saville of the Museum of the American Indian asked whether I could possibly find him a copy of the reprint. I had no hope whatever of success, but promised to try anyway.

After a three-hour session with Mr. Aiken of John Grant's, I wandered down the street and paused by the shilling stand of a neighboring shop. There was a brand-new copy of the primer in a paper wrapper.

It really looked too good to be true. I therefore took my friend inside the shop, handed over my bob, and asked the proprietor if he had any more copies, because I would like to buy them all.

He went into the back room, poked around, and returned with the news that he had 172 copies, on which he would make me a special rate of sixpence a volume. This broke the market in Indian primers, so that I was able to pay only a measly half of my trip to Europe from the proceeds.

In the early part of this century one of the most celebrated publishers of limited editions in America was Elbert Hubbard of East Aurora, New York. He called his plant the Roycroft Shop, and made a great to-do about handwork and tiny editions. Hubbard was the first – and, I trust, the last – person who ever succeeded in persuading anybody to buy a book in ooze calf leather.

Hubbard went down with the *Titanic.* Only a few days before he sailed, I had lunch with him at the Savarin Restaurant in Penn Station.

"Mr. Hubbard," I said, "you put out a book recently in an edition strictly limited to a hundred copies. So far, I have personally seen a hundred and fifteen copies. How about it?"

Hubbard grinned. "Oh, those are limited to a hundred copies for each state."

The man from whom Hubbard probably stole most of his ideas about bookmaking (except for the ooze leather, which was original) was an interesting character of a very different type, Thomas Bird Mosher, of Portland, Maine. Mosher had a delicate, *fin-de-siècle* taste in literature, and introduced such people as Lionel Johnson and William Ernest Henley to America in dainty little volumes almost invariably printed from hand-set type on Van Gelder handmade paper. His editions, though not individually numbered, were really limited: after each printing he would have the type distributed, and if there was enough demand for a second edition, he would start all over again.

Anyone who expected, after timidly fondling a vellum Mosher edition of William Morris or Fiona Macleod, to find Tom Mosher himself an Aubrey Beardsley type would have been sorely mistaken. He was a burly figure with a walrus mustache, reputed among his friends to be the most profane man in the book trade. Unfortunately I never met him in that mood; I would have liked to draw comparisons.

Hubbard prepared himself for publishing by working as advertising manager of a Buffalo soap works; Mosher's literary taste was formed before the mast of his father's square-rigger. At fourteen he sailed around the world, and his father gave him a set of *Bell's British Theatre* to occupy the off watches. By chance, John Bell (who published the *Theatre*) was more of an influence on English bookmaking than on book contents – the set, after all, was a reprint of the classics. And Tom Mosher absorbed a feel for how books should look that never left him.

After a brief turn in a law stationery and publishing business in Portland, Mosher borrowed three thousand dollars (from a friend who said, "This is all I have, and I'll never see it back, but go ahead") and set up as a publisher in 1893 with the issue of George Meredith's *Modern Love*. He sold almost all his books by mail (from his catalogue) to individual buyers.

He paid royalties to his American authors; most of the English ones he pirated, the American copyright law in those days being on his side. Andrew Lang and some other victims were very angry. Others said just as loudly that without Mosher they would never have been known in America.

Two things distinguished Mosher as a publisher, aside from his unerring, though rather precious, taste: he was probably the first in this country who was, and made other people, conscious of books as physical things; and he made a great deal of money doing it. He found a way of turning taste and personality into cash that has been the despair of "fine-book lovers" in the trade ever since.

In 1898 my store was at 18 East 21st Street. One night as I was getting ready to leave, a tremendous man walked in, priced a book, and bought it. He said as he handed me the money, "Old books aren't worth a damn."

Nobody in those days could have failed to recognize Thomas B. Reed, of Portland, Maine, "the czar of Congress." By this time he was out of office and practising law in New York.

"Mr. Reed," said I, "when old books are intelligently bought, they sometimes make a very good investment."

"Oh, hell," he said, "my law library in Portland cost me thousands, and when I left, I had to sell it for fifty dollars."

"I don't believe you heard me, Mr. Reed. I said when old books were intelligently bought."

The whole store shook with his laughter.

From then on Mr. Reed used to drop in at the store occasionally. Once when he was there, John Finley brought in Reverend Henry Van Dyke, and the three of them sat in the back room swapping stories. Mr. Reed told about his first New York law practice. A railroad gave him a case, which he immediately settled out of court. Falling into conversation with a fellow lawyer from an adjoining office, he remarked that he had put in about two hours' work on the job, and was trying to work up nerve to send a bill for five hundred dollars.

"Just let me have one of your billheads," said the neighbor.

Within a week Mr. Reed had a check for $5000 and an effusive letter of thanks from the railroad.

When I first knew John Finley, he had just come to New York, after being the youngest college president in America, at Knox College in Galesburg, Illinois. Knox College had one of the best collections of Americana in the Midwest, practically all of which was presented to it by Edward Caldwell, then the president of the McGraw-Hill Publishing Company.

This takes me back to a stranger who came into my store on 33rd Street and announced that he wanted to buy every book in existence about Louisiana.

I dug out my *Century Atlas,* showed him Louisiana before the Purchase, and said I guessed he could accomplish his object if he had about five million dollars.

He said he was really more interested in the Mississippi River, and hoped he could do it with twenty-five thousand.

I told him he could make a very good start.

He bought several expensive books then and there, and came in every week for the next six months. He was a retired engineer by the name of Preston Player.

Then I saw nothing of him for a couple of years. One day the phone rang, and he asked me down to lunch with him at Tenth Street. His collection had got to the point where he thought it should be insured, and he wanted me to appraise it. As I had sold him practically everything he had, the appraisal was only an hour's work. He asked me what he owed, and I said, "Mr. Player, you bought ninety per cent of this from me, and I might better ask you what I owe you."

There was another interval of silence, this one lasting three years. Again he asked me to lunch. This time he said, "Everitt, I'm going to die in three or four days, and I want to know what to do with my books. Whom shall I give them to?"

"That's one question I won't answer. All I can tell you is, give them to a small institution, not a big one."

"Why so?"

I explained that large libraries in the Mississippi Valley region would surely have at least 75 per cent of the choice items, so that the gift would really be wasted. With this I departed. Soon afterwards I saw Mr. Player's obituary, but I had no idea where the books were going.

Six months later Mr. Caldwell, who was also an old and valued customer of mine, sent me a catalogue of the books presented to Knox College by Preston Player. I scanned the catalogue eagerly, then hurried to the telephone.

"Thanks a lot for the catalogue, Mr. Caldwell," I said. "It's a damn good job, but you've been to the circus and missed seeing the elephants."

"What do you mean?"

"The best single thing Player had isn't in the catalogue."

"Well, we put in everything that was there."

I said, "Mr. Caldwell, do you know Meyer's *Universum*?"

"Of course I do – who doesn't? The volume of the American views is common enough. Mr. Player wouldn't have been very proud of having that."

"No," I said, "but Goodspeed sold him the original painting from which the engraving of Nauvoo in 1843 was made."

This news threw Mr. Caldwell into considerable excitement. Nauvoo was the place on the Mississippi where the Mormons settled after they had migrated from Kirkland, Ohio. Angry neighbors finally ran the Mormon settlers out of Nauvoo, killing the prophet, Joseph Smith, in the process. The Mormons made one more settlement, in Zion, Missouri, before they finally set out for Utah.

At all events, Mr. Caldwell said there was no painting of Nauvoo in the Player collection.

"There was when I appraised it; I put five hundred dollars on it," I said.

Mr. Caldwell maαe tracks for the storage warehouse where the Player collection had been temporarily housed. As is customary in such cases, the warehouse people vowed they had faithfully delivered every single scrap in the Player collection, and there had never been any painting. On his way out,

Mr. Caldwell poked a toe at some dusty paintings stacked against a wall with their backs out. "What about those?"

"Oh, that's junk we're about to throw away. We couldn't get a starting bid of a dollar for it last week."

Covered with grime, Mr. Caldwell emerged some minutes later clutching the painting of Nauvoo to his bosom.

The next time I saw Mr. Caldwell, he had the painting under his arm. "I'm going to take a train to Galesburg and deliver this picture personally to Knox College." And so he did.

Booksellers, like some of my other friends, are always boasting about their successes; their mistakes they somehow find less colorful.

I have made at least one mistake colorful enough to go in this book. The American Art Association catalogued in one of its sales "a map of Mexico, Louisiana and the Missouri Territory, including also the State of Mississippi, Alabama Territory, East and West Florida, Georgia, South Carolina and Part of the Island of Cuba. By John H. Robinson, M.D. Member of the Military Philosophical Society of America, Member of the Western Museum Society of Cincinnati, and Brigr. General in the Republican armies of Mexico &c. . . . Engd. by J. Anderson, Philada. Copyright secured according to law. A.D. 1819. Printed and Coloured by John L. Narstin of Philadelphia."

I knew nothing about it, but decided I was going to buy it. Even blind, I was sure it would cost me $250.

At the sale somebody yelled ten dollars, and I said twelve and a half, and down came the hammer. Eberstadt and half the other bright lights of Americana were in the room watching, but this distinguished company was supplied to me at no extra cost. The map meant nothing to them, and they were thinking about something else. When I got the map back to the store, where I was by then in very cramped quarters (having discovered that the fat books just fill shelves and the thin ones bring you the money), I tried to open the map, but since it was over five and a half feet square, all I could look at was one uninteresting corner.

I was contemplating this without enthusiasm when Ed Eberstadt came in. "What you got there, Charlie?"

"Oh, I don't know. I can't get the damn thing open."

"What'll you take for it?"

"Well, I was going up to two hundred and fifty. It's yours for seventy-five."

Ed paid and departed. Ed's office was even smaller than mine. He too was just trying to inform himself when Philip Ashton Rollins, a truly great collector of Western Americana, over a million dollars' worth of which he gave to Princeton, came into the store.

"Ed, what was that thing Charlie bought yesterday?"

"Don't know; I'm just trying to find out."

"What will you sell it to me for?"

"I gave Charlie seventy-five dollars; take it for a hundred."

Shortly after this, word of the transaction got around, as word always does. My friend and customer Tom Streeter called up and said, "Charlie, I kind of think you made a mistake on that map. There are only two other copies in existence, and the Library of Congress has both."

Tom promptly went down and traded some of his duplicates to the Library of Congress for their spare. Possibly the point of this story is that Mr. Rollins, being a rich man, had a sleigh bed big enough to unfold the map all the way.

Philip Ashton Rollins wrote *The Cowboy*, the outstanding

and, in fact, unique book on the subject, and edited some rare Western travels. He has always been one of my favorite customers.

The first time I saw him he came into the store on 34th Street from an exceedingly gay party. I didn't know him from the man in the moon. "I'll buy any damn thing that mentions a cowboy," was his introductory remark.

"Covers quite a lot of territory, doesn't it?" I asked cautiously.

"All right, try me."

I hooked out this and that and the other from the shelves.

He didn't pick and choose; he said, not quite crisply, "How much?"

I ran up the total on an adding machine: $1243.

"All right, let me have 'em."

He went over to my packing table, tore a strip off my roll of manila wrapping paper, and wrote out a check on one of the large trust companies for $1243.

If this had not been during banking hours, I can't imagine what I should have done. As it was, the head office of the Manufacturers' Trust was across the street, and I skipped over to see Mr. Jonas, then president.

"Mr. Jonas," I said, "I think this is probably just a practical joke. Would you look at this so-called check?"

Jonas looked, put in a phone call, and came back grinning. "I wish I had a few more like that," he said. "This guy keeps a regular balance in the hundreds of thousands."

Afterward I got to wondering what had originally interested Rollins in the cowboy; finally I knew him well enough to ask.

"Well," he said, "I guess everybody knows my father left me hundreds of thousands of acres and several banks and things in the West. Those didn't last very long. Then another relative died and contributed another injection, but that didn't last, either.

"When the First World War came along, I decided I wasn't good for anything but cannon fodder, but the American army said I was too old. So I sneaked into the Anzacs. I had quite a rough time, and some of my Aussie friends pulled me out of the line of fire more than once.

"Evenings in billets I used to amuse them by telling about the cowboys back home, some of whom had done me the same sort of favor.

"Finally one long, lanky Anzac got fed up: 'Phil, you're a lousy son of a bitch. You keep telling us how cowboys were always saving your life, but you don't do anything about it.' So I came home from the war without a dime, and made tracks for the West to straighten myself out. I got a job on a ranch that I had once owned, digging postholes at two bits a hole.

"As I was digging away to beat hell, trying to make a showing, a party of dudes came by. So I married one of the dudes, who was just as much interested in cowboys as I was, and whose father owned about half of some eastern state."

I don't feel quite so much bruised about my mistake over the Robinson map because I can comfort myself by remembering what befell my almost infallible friend Mike Walsh of Goodspeed's. His catalogue Number 168, 1927, was among the most interesting I have ever seen. In the midst of looking through it, I picked up the telephone and called Boston. "Mike, have you still got Number 2211?"

"No. Sorry; it's gone. How much did I slip on that?"

"Plenty," said I, reluctantly hanging up.

One of the prime rarities of Western Americana is *The Nez Percé's First Book,* one of eight little schoolbooks printed at Clearwater, Idaho, on a press that some missionaries brought across the ocean and up the mountains from Hawaii in 1839.

When I appraised the Coe collection, I put a value of fifteen hundred dollars on the copy of the book there.

Some years ago, the last time I was in Oregon, I found to my great surprise that Hines, one of the earliest Oregon printers, was still active. I ran into him at the Oregon Historical Society.

"Do you know whatever became of that Clearwater Mission press, Mr. Hines?" I asked.

"You're leaning againt it."

Hines, who was in his nineties, loved to talk. That day he told me about a stranger who came into the printing office with some poetry. He said, "Set these up," gave his name as Joaquin Miller, and departed, never to be seen again.

Before he knew Miller was not coming back, Hines, lacking a title for the poetry, scribbled "Specimens" across the top of the manuscript, set it, and pulled two proofs.

He kept them long enough so that one proof was worth five hundred dollars to Fred Skiff, whose copy I later bought and resold to Mr. Huntington. Heavens knows what became of the other one; but anyhow I have shaken the hand that set Joaquin Miller's first printed verses.

I have also shaken the hand of the bard himself. For a while I had charge of the first retail store Doubleday opened at Fifth Avenue and 28th Street. An old man in a red shirt, with long white hair, walked in and looked around. There was no mistaking him in those days. "What can I do for you, Mr. Miller?" said I.

I was a total stranger to him, but any admiring audience brought him out. "I've never seen the City Hall," he said.

"All right, let's go see it." I started for the subway, which apparently shocked him.

"No, no, I want to walk."

So for the one time in my life I walked from 28th Street to City Hall, talking with the old man and inspecting new buildings, half-finished buildings, and excavations for intended buildings.

After we had reached our goal, Miller said, "I don't want to see any more of this town. It has more holes in the ground than any mining camp I was ever in." And that was my experience with Joaquin Miller.

Even the best people in the business sometimes forget or are hurried into overlooking things. My friend Charlie Harris, of Edwards's Bookshop in London, about as learned a bookseller as I know, once paid fifty pounds at an auction for a set of *Cook's Voyages*, printed in New York.

The only feature that makes this set really worth more than fifty cents is that it contains two plates engraved by Paul Revere, and when Charlie inspected his purchase, he found that the engravings were missing.

I have remarked before that nothing ever turns up singly. Just a few days later I was in Edinburgh, and after a day's hunting I passed by the store of a dealer I particularly disliked, and found him arranging his stock for the next day.

Among the junk was a ruinous copy of *Cook's Voyages*, with practically nothing left of it except the engravings neatly signed Paul Revere.

"How much for this?" I asked. I knew as well as he did that he was laying out his shilling table.

"Ten bob," said he.

"Go to hell, you Scotch robber," I observed, and stamped on down the hill.

But as I went, I began thinking about Michael O'Shaughnessy, the New York dealer and auctioneer. I had once encountered him just after he had given a piece of his mind to a Fourth Avenue dealer. When I met him, he was mumbling assorted curses.

"What's the matter, O'Shaughnessy?" I asked.

"Oh, I'm just cursing myself for a damn fool. I've made up my mind that from now on any dealer is welcome to spit in my eye and rub it in with his foot, so long as I get a bargain."

O'Shaughnessy's words of wisdom prevailed; I turned back, and, perhaps not very graciously, flung a ten-shilling note at the Scotsman. I removed the engravings from the book, then I dropped the book into the nearest dustbin.

Back in London I went to see Charlie Harris, looking as innocent as I knew how. "Charlie," I said, "I hate to see a pal get stuck. It wasn't really your fault you came a cropper on *Cook's Voyages,* and maybe I could take it off your hands."

Charlie looked at me quizzically. "You son of a bitch, I bet you have the Revere plates."

"Right here in my pocket," I said.

"You'll take ten quid for it, and think yourself lucky," said Charlie.

And so I did.

On one of my early visits to London, I was warned by all hands against a bookseller named Jackson, in Charing Cross Road. He was notorious for hating Yankees.

All the London bookshops in those days closed at seven o'clock, so about six-fifty I went into Jackson's and said, "I hear you don't like Yankees. Will you have a beer with me?"

"That far I'll go," he said.

I kept at this until about the fifth time, Jackson said, "Would you pay me fifty pounds for a fine copy of *Simcoe's Journal?*"

I said I would be glad to. So he took me downstairs to look

at the Americana. He had five or six shelves of very choice rarities. They were so reasonably priced that my only problem was whether to buy just some or all.

I added up my purchases and said, "Here, I'll write you a check."

"No damn Yankee can buy books from me that way," he rejoined.

"Well, how must I do it?"

"I'll send the books to your hotel; if you like them, you send me a draft; if you don't, send them back."

As we were going up the stairs, I noticed a red leather volume labeled *Autographs*. I put my hand on it.

"Here, no damn Yankee can look at that," he said, so I took my hand away.

I came for another visit the following year. Then I skipped a year. Two years afterward I was received by Jackson's son.

"Where's your dad?" I asked.

"He died three months ago," said Jackson, junior. "Weren't you and he dickering about some volume of autographs?"

"Dickering, hell! He wouldn't even let me look at it."

Young Jackson fetched the volume out—a dazzling red morocco folio. True to his father's principles, he did not open it. "Would you give me five pounds for it?"

"Glad to," I said, and that was the last I saw of my mysterious purchase until it and I were back in New York.

Just as I was leafing through it, trying to find out what I had, Roger Howson, then the librarian of Columbia University, came in. He asked what I had there.

"I'm just trying to find out," I said. We sat down together to look. It turned out that the volume contained secret documents relating to an early-nineteenth-century treaty among Great Britain, France, and Belgium. The secrecy was so grave that none of the diplomats involved signed his real name to the papers; but the volume had belonged to one of those present, who added a key at the back of the book. Howson offered me $750 for the book, and I stalled him off. I put it under a counter where I hoped no one would notice it. I should have known better, considering my experience with book people.

Shortly my prize customer, Albert W. Johnston, came in and rapidly piled up an order for several hundred dollars. He pounced on the projecting bright red edge of the autograph book. "What's this?"

I said hell, I didn't know. It was no use; Johnston went through the book from cover to cover. "What's this worth?"

"I haven't the slightest idea; I don't want to price it at all. The librarian of Columbia offered me seven hundred and fifty, and I wouldn't let him have it."

Johnston was a man of decision. "All right, you can sell me this, or you can forget the rest of this order." So he got the autograph book for $750.

During the recent war conscience began to trouble him. He thought the documents belonged in Britain, so he sent his daughter down to the British Ambassador.

"I'll be glad to accept these on behalf of a grateful nation," said the diplomat, suavely.

"Oh, you don't know Dad," said Johnston's daughter. "He won't take your receipt. This has to go to Winston Churchill personally, and only his receipt will do."

The papers are in England now, and Johnston has his receipt and a personal note from Winston Churchill, which I imagine he values even more than the documents he gave up.

On one of my periodic trips to London, my friend Leon Kashnor, of the Museum Book Shop, said, "Look out, Charlie.

Someone in the Hudson's Bay Company has been dumping stuff. I don't know where it's gone to, but look out."

Two years later I was back in London and stopped in at Foyle's Book Shop. The Americana department is on the third floor. Some boys were carrying in piles of stuff.

"What's this?" I asked the manager.

"Oh, some junk we bought from the Hudson's Bay Company."

"Have you priced it yet?"

"No."

"What would you do if I picked out a hundred volumes right now?"

"Well, I guess you can pick out a hundred volumes for six bob apiece."

I sat down on the floor and started picking, trembling in every limb for fear one of the owners should come upstairs. My nerves got the better of me after I had picked 181 books. "How about these?" I asked.

"Well, Charlie, I didn't think you'd pick out quite so many," said the Americana expert. "For this quantity, how about five bob each? Shall I put them on your bill?"

"I guess I'd better pay you right now," I said, "because I have a shipment going off tomorrow, and I'd like to have these delivered across the street today." So I paid up, got a receipted bill, and fled across the street to Marks & Company before any of the Foyles should turn up.

I opened my packages in the presence of Mr. Marks and his partner Mark Cohen, one of the two or three most learned booksellers in London. Each time that I picked up a volume, Mr. Cohen remarked succinctly, "Charlie, you son of a bitch."

* * *

In the course of my trips to London I found that for some reason it was almost always a single dealer, even a single purchase, that paid for my whole trip. One of the nicest booksellers I have ever known was old George Suckling, an outstanding specialist in English literature. I used to go to his store just for the pleasure of talking to him, though this was rendered rather more difficult by the necessity of shouting through a tin ear trumpet.

One day I said, "George, have you got any Americana?"

"Oh, I don't think so — maybe a few oddments down cellar."

The oddment corner was lit by about a ten-watt bulb.

A thing every bookseller dreads is finding several copies of one title. It practically always means junk that won't even move off the dime counter. But for some reason, even though there were two copies of a dull-looking little book labeled, *Report of Milton and Cheadle,* I gave a second glance. Milton and Cheadle were two Englishmen who had been sent to western North America in the 1850's. Their book on what they saw is a standard source for Northwestern history, and worth about three dollars and a half. Before they published this, they were unreliably alleged to have presented a special report to Parliament. No copy had ever been found.

These two copies, barely visible in the dim light, were proof that the report had been made. George Suckling had neatly penciled in his price, five shillings each.

I went upstairs. "You're wrong on these," I said. "You've got them marked five bob, but I'll be glad to give you ten quid each."

"Charlie," said George, "if I'm so ignorant that I mark a ten-pound book five shillings, the price to you is five bob less ten per cent."

Aside from the secrecy of the report, these rarities had no

great value compared to that of the normal three-fifty book; but each of the two copies fetched a dollar for every cent that the latter books commanded.

The last time I saw George Suckling was shortly before his death. I had spent a rather unprofitable three weeks in England and was sailing on the *Aquitania* in the afternoon. I had saved up two or three hours for a social chat with George.

"George," I bellowed through the ear trumpet, "nobody has paid for my trip this year."

"That's a shame, Charlie," said George. He turned to his son George and said, "Didn't we put something aside for Charlie last year?"

George Junior went downstairs, no doubt to contend with the ten-watt bulb. Finally he returned with a quarto volume wrapped in paper. "Charlie," said the old man, "before you open this, I warn you it's going to cost you ten guineas." From the size, it might have been any one of several two-dollar books that I hoped it was not, or it might just possibly have been *Simcoe's Journal,* worth five hundred dollars on a good day, which I hoped it was.

Instead, it was the first copy I had ever seen of Goldson's *Northwest Passage,* privately printed in a small edition at Portsmouth in 1793.

"George," I said, as I pulled out my checkbook, "somebody did pay for my trip, after all."

I took my prize over to Henry Stevens, Son and Stiles, who keep a record of every book they have ever sold since the 1840's. Henry Stevens, III, admitted that they had never sold but one copy. I resisted his efforts to buy mine, and finally got six hundred from Dr. Rosenbach for it.

Ten years later a copy of the Goldson book came up for sale at Sotheby's, the only copy ever sold at auction. Vilhjalmur

Stefansson, the arctic explorer, one of my best friends and customers, asked me what he would have to bid to get this for his collection. I told him he would be lucky if he got it for sixty pounds. So he mortgaged the old homestead, and sent a bid of three hundred dollars.

When the book reached him, there was a bill with it for twenty pounds.

(I got back some of my own, when I appraised the Stefansson collection, by putting a figure of $750 on the book.)

You know the axiom about antiquities; when no copy is known to exist, and somebody discovers one, it is never a matter of more than a year or two before further copies come to light. My *Milton and Cheadle* was just one instance, although usually the first discovery does not occur in duplicate.

The best buys almost always come from the big shops who are not scared to death by rare items rather than from the obscure little shops where the inexperienced book-hunter would naturally look for rarities at dirt-cheap prices. I went into Dutton's bookstore on Fifth Avenue and asked the manager of the rare-book department, a cocky little Englishman named Grant, if he had any Americana.

"You know we don't deal in that junk," he replied severely. "There's some stuff on the floor over there, and you can have any of that you want at fifty cents a volume."

I've always refused to be insulted, so I sat down on the floor and began looking through the junk. All I found in the pile was a copy of George Meredith's *The Shaving of Shagpat*. This copy had been defaced by a two-page inscription signed "George," so our great authority had priced it at fifty cents.

(This I sold to another dealer for three-fifty—$350, of course.)

Then I picked up an item issued in a limited edition by the Marine Research Society. I showed it to Grant.

"Oh, that damn thing," he said. "We've been looking for the limited edition for three months, but that trade edition you can have for two dollars."

After allowing a suitable time to elapse, I quoted Mr. Grant the limited edition at sixty-five dollars, and he eagerly bought it back from me.

My life has revolved around Americana, but you can see I have had some fun with other books as well. One day in the 1920's I was going into Thorpe's bookstore in St. Martin's Lane in London as the manager was helping an old lady into her carriage.

"Hello, Charlie," said he. "Do you know who that was? Thackeray's daughter, Lady Ritchie."

"What have you been buying from her?" I asked.

"Oh, just a lot of rubbish."

"Let me see it," I said.

Rubbish was no word for it. There were several hundred volumes of absolute shelf-warmers.

My eye fell on the least promising of the lot, a little duodecimo Greek Testament. I found it was scrawled full of notes in Thackeray's unmistakable hand, which anyone who has once seen it can recognize across the room. He had also drawn a map in ink.

"Duke," I said to Thorpe's manager, "what did you pay for this junk?"

"Fifty quid," he told me.

"All right, how much for this Testament?"

"That's the only book in the lot."

"All right, all right, how much?"

"Seventy-five quid."

"I'll take it," I said. I thought I had a customer in mind, which is always the first thing a sensible bookseller does when he starts spending money rashly.

My first act the next day was to read up on Thackeray's life. I found he had been refused entrance to Cambridge because he had had no Greek. He spent six months at his uncle's studying Greek, obviously from this New Testament, because here were all his cramming notes.

My friends in the London book trade had sudden fits of compassion about the extravagant price I had paid for the Testament. One of them offered to take over half of my risk, and two others each offered me a hundred pounds to get me clear of my predicament.

Owen Young was one of perhaps a dozen great Thackeray collectors at the time, and I wrote and told him I had something he needed.

He wrote back: "I have all the Thackeray I ever want to see."

I wrote across the face of his reply: "You ain't seen nothing yet." A week later he owned the book, at a price that paid my passage to England and back.

On that same trip I also exercised my shrewdness, to considerably less purpose, in buying Americana. One of Sotheby's auction catalogues listed a thirty-two-page manuscript, by an unknown hand, describing an Indian battle in the West. My friend Leon Kashnor, of the Museum Book Store, and I fixed our eagle eyes on this and jointly bought it for ninety pounds, over spirited bidding from the firm of Henry Stevens. I dressed up our prize with a twenty-dollar morocco slip case from Zaehnsdorf's, and took it home to make a killing.

Apparently I was the only dealer in America who had not

seen and refrained from buying this manuscript when Charles Goodspeed originally catalogued it for $150. Some years later, by high-pressure salesmanship, I unloaded my prize for $125.

The bête noire of every American bookseller, and particularly of those who deal by mail, is probably the newspapers. Every time a newspaper lacks three-quarters of an inch at the bottom of a column, it sticks in an item to the effect that Mrs. Sally Jones has in her possession a copy of the *Ulster County Gazette* printed at Kingston, New York, in 1800, containing an obituary notice of George Washington; and she has refused five hundred dollars for it.

Mail-order dealers always have more correspondence than they can handle anyway, and after one of these tidbits in the papers the mail doubles or triples. Even now, when I am more or less trying to pull my hole in after me, I get at least two letters a week about the accursed *Ulster County Gazette.*

In the first place, I have never understood why everyone had to have this particular obituary of Washington when three hundred other hick-town papers printed similar ones. And in the second place, Mr. R. W. G. Vail (then at the New York Public Library) devoted an entire pamphlet to the reprint of this particular notorious issue.

When an old lady brings one of the reprints to the store, the routine is invariable. She spreads the paper out with trembling hands, and explains that it must have been in the family for at least a hundred years because her grandmother lived to be ninety and had inherited the treasure from *her* grandmother.

Ninety-nine out of every hundred copies I see are among the quarter-million or so printed as souvenirs to be given away at the Philadelphia Centennial Exposition of 1876. I have developed a very keen eye for this particular reprint, but it has done me less than no good.

For years I would try to explain the true state of affairs to each hopeful owner. I finally gave up when the twentieth old lady said, "Can you suggest anyone who *knows something* about old newspapers?" Now I find it simpler to lie and say I don't buy old newspapers.

Another newspaper bane of booksellers' lives is the *Vicksburg Gazette*. It is usually offered to me as "the first Confederate newspaper printed on wallpaper." A more detailed yarn is that the particular issue in question was printed while Grant was besieging Vicksburg, so that nothing but wallpaper was available to the printer. This, too, was reprinted for a souvenir, and many, many thousands were given away. The routine on this one, of course, is, "My great-grandfather was in Grant's army, and got one of these copies when Vicksburg fell."

Among the most valuable forms of information to historians is the city directory. You can judge the standing of the first New York City directory when I tell you that a copy came up at auction some years ago, and a prosperous Bronx real-estate dealer commissioned me to buy it for him up to $3000.

I bought it in for $2750. My old pals the newspapermen ran a story about this.

Then came the deluge. Not one but five hundred people wrote, telegraphed, and telephoned to advise me that they had directories of New York City at least a hundred years old. Of course they did not expect to get $2750, but they thought a modest figure like $1000 might interest me.

It was no use telling them that New York directories of the nineteenth century, useful as they may be to historians, are properly bought by the bushel, not the piece, so about all I could say was that my directory needs were already supplied.

An even worse scourge than the *Ulster County Gazette* and directories is old Bibles.

In the Robert Hoe sale, George D. Smith paid fifty thousand dollars for a Gutenberg Bible, and naturally was smeared all over the front pages for doing so.

At that time there were 130,000,000 people in the United States, and judging from my correspondence in the succeeding six months, every man, woman, and child of the lot owned a priceless Bible over a hundred years old, usually in German.

Naturally it was not my luck to be offered any of the German Bibles printed by Christopher Sower in Germantown, which are sometimes worth as much as fifty dollars; no, all I drew was the output of the Lutherans and the American Bible Society, which was founded for the express purpose of giving Bibles away free.

The only standard American Bible I know of that is worth any real money is the first English Bible issued in this country, printed by Robert Aitkin of Philadelphia in 1782. Of course there were many testaments and psalm books before that. I have had my hands on one copy, which was offered to me by an old gun dealer for three hundred dollars.

Bibles are very hard books to collate (to check for missing pages or plates, that is), because the older ones seldom have any page numbers, and you practically have to read the Good Book straight through to make sure nothing is gone. In this case I gave my friend Seymour Dunbar twenty-five dollars to do a thorough job on the Aitkin Bible.

Four days later he brought it back with a note saying that it was all perfect, probably the best copy ever offered.

On the strength of this I sold the book to a collector for $750.

A week or two later the new owner came in grinning and

said, "I've just been collating that Bible again, and it lacks forty-two pages."

I was resigned to writing this off as a loss, but some weeks later apparently God looked after His own because I came upon another defective copy that had the pages I lacked. In this way I was able to make up a complete copy, but the total cost, including what the English call a "shiny" binding, turned my original $450 profit into a $25 loss.

One queer character in the book trade was in his day one of the best known dealers, Gabriel Wells. When I first knew him, his name was Gabriel Weiss, and he was peddling some set of subscription books around Sussex County, New Jersey. A little later he had a grisly furnished room on Lexington Avenue. He once came into my store on 23rd Street and said, "If I don't sell some books, I don't eat." So I went up with him to his room, and paid him $3.65 for some of his stock, to provide him with the next day's meals.

Then for years he eked out a living by going around to various bookstores, picking out some set on approval for thirty dollars and selling it to Macy's for thirty-five.

Finally he inherited a large amount of money from some relative. You wouldn't have known old Gabe. He went to London, rented one of the swellest apartments he could find, and made abundant use of the unlimited credit that the big London booksellers used to give for approval shipments in those days.

(The first time I went to the famous bookshop of Maggs Brothers, Mr. Ernest Maggs took me to lunch, said that Gabriel Wells had recommended me, and told me that if I wanted to use it, I might have up to a hundred thousand pounds of credit for books on approval. I said I was just a little piker that liked to buy books and pay for them – one of the most foolish statements I have ever made in the course of a foolish life.)

Mrs. Everitt and I arrived in London at the time of the general strike, and found at our hotel several messages asking me to call Gabriel Wells. When I did so, he invited us to dinner at Simpson's. All through the evening he was very careful to talk about nothing in particular. Going home in a cab, he casually pulled out some manuscripts and asked if I wasn't going to Birmingham. I said I expected to be passing that way.

Wells explained that he had paid Lowe of Birmingham four hundred pounds for these alleged Goldsmith letters, that he was leaving for home in two days, that he thought they were forgeries, and that he hoped I wouldn't mind doing him the small favor of throwing the letters back at the seller.

I was too much taken aback to say anything, but all night I got madder and madder. Wells knew perfectly well that the vendor would not take back the fakes, but he thought if I was buying enough stuff, maybe I could get away with it.

In the morning I returned the letters with a note to Wells saying that I had changed my itinerary.

These forgeries were part of the output of a very remarkable Englishman. He was a historian, the author of several standard works. When he was not writing history, he used to write Shelley, Goldsmith, and General Wolfe letters better than the old boys had ever dreamed of in their lifetimes. He was much more careful about it than such bunglers as Thomas J. Wise, and always got contemporary paper. His products were really almost worth the price for the art they displayed. A prominent British dealer gave him fifty pounds for a beautiful Shelley letter, and then sold it for five hundred. The dealer, being a man of conscience, called him in, said he had done a little better than he had expected, and handed over another hundred pounds.

Two days later the buyer returned the letter as a forgery.

Finally so much of this went on that the authorities did as they sometimes do in this country when a corporation is too big to be allowed to go bankrupt: they simply hinted that such an artist would be better off in some other country, and he forthwith retired to Paris.

The last I heard of him was a letter in which he ordered six hundred dollars' worth of books. I replied, starchily, that I would be glad to ship them on receipt of draft.

I have seldom been so stunned as I was when I got a draft from him by return mail.

Stevenson's *The Ebb Tide,* which he wrote in collaboration with his stepson, Lloyd Osbourne, is dedicated to one of the McClures. I was closing up my store on 34th Street one day when this McClure came in and said, "Here's the original manuscript of *The Ebb Tide*. I've been lugging it around with me wherever I went all over the country, and I'm sick of it. I'd rather have five dollars than this damned manuscript."

"Here's the five dollars," I said. "Come back day after tomorrow, and I'll have some more money for you."

"There are several chapters missing from the manuscript, you know," McClure said.

"Natural enough," I said "because Osbourne wrote quite a bit of the book."

Next morning I took the manuscript to Gabriel Wells, who laid fifteen hundred dollars on the line without batting an eye. I gave half of this to McClure, and we were both quite pleased.

Wells, never a man to let grass grow under his feet, hunted up Lloyd Osbourne, who was still alive, and gave him five hundred dollars to write out in longhand the chapters he had originally contributed to the book. That completed the manuscript, and raised the ultimate sales price to what was unreliably reported as ten thousand dollars.

Another peculiar character who frequented rare-bookstores was not a dealer but a customer, Charlie Montgomery, of Brooklyn. His mania was the Baconian controversy, and he used to go around with a reprint of the Shakespeare First Folio, for which he had out a series of cardboard masks, showing which words on each page were the cipher that proved Bacon had written Shakespeare's plays.

The last time I saw Charlie, John Anderson of the Anderson Galleries was in the store, too.

"John," said Charlie, "I want you to do something for me. I can't travel by boat, because I get terribly seasick. But I know you can do this. Just go and dig up Shakespeare's grave, and I'm certain you will find documents to prove that Bacon wrote the plays."

"How's this again, Charlie?" John Anderson asked.

"Why, all you have to do is take a boat and a couple of men up the Thames, and you can dig up the grave as easy as nothing."

"Charlie, did you ever hear of Scotland Yard?"

"Why, John, they wouldn't ever bother *you!*"

I am now going to tackle an impossible job – to give some idea of George D. Smith, the great book merchant. I said before that he was the greatest we have ever had in this country. He never read anything but an occasional racing form; his word was said to be better than his checks, which sometimes bounced; he died at the one time in his life when he was worth a million dollars. Once when I went to the race track with him I found that he thought less of betting five thousand dollars than I did of plunging a two-spot.

George reached his position fundamentally because of two things. The first was that (except when he didn't feel like paying his bills) money meant absolutely nothing to him. Most of us, when we attend an auction, pencil in a price we are willing to go to on the items we want. Not George. He just put a check mark, which meant that not J. P. Morgan himself stood any chance of buying the items at the sale. (If you looked over his shoulder and saw the check against something your heart was set on and said, "George, will you lay off that?" he would invariably do so.)

George once said to me, "Charlie, you're absolutely crazy. You deal every day with men who think in thousands, and you talk in five-dollar bills." George never made that mistake; this was one of his two secrets.

The other, which he shared with every great bookseller, was his memory. He knew offhand at an auction the price for which any other copy of any consequential book on the block had sold.

George was a plunger in business as well as at the track. He very seldom had any orders for items he bought at sales. And since it was absolutely immaterial to him what he paid, he often found himself with high-priced enigmas on the shelves. His method with such special customers as Henry E. Huntington was to show them the auction bill and say, "Here, I paid five hundred for this; it's yours for five hundred and fifty."

Sometimes, when he bought a book from a scout for a hundred dollars, he would insist on a receipted bill for three hundred. (George did not invent this method of taking profits, which has been used by other hungry dealers before and since.)

By his prominence, his prices, his success, and his personality, George established himself as the last word on book prices among scouts. I remember once a traveling salesman who used to bring me in a good many bargains, turned up with a bound volume of sheet music, seven of the items bearing Abraham Lincoln's signature. He asked me $500. They weren't worth it, and I was shyly thinking of $250, but for the sake of politeness I asked, "Would you take any less?"

"No," said the salesman, and went over to George Smith.

George was always sitting at his desk, looking more than half asleep. He glanced up. "How much?" he mumbled, practically unintelligibly.

"Five hundred dollars," repeated the salesman.

"Man, you're absolutely nuts! I'll give you one hundred!"

When George said so, you just took the money and beat it.

Here is a story that leads back to George in the end. I was at Leary, Stuart's store in Philadelphia, in the office of Warner, the Americana man. He said, "Have you ever been to see C. W. Unger down in Pottsville?"

"Never heard of him," I said.

"Well, he has quite a lot of curious Americana in his house. You ought to go down some time."

One morning I found myself confronted with a day in Philadelphia. I had once spent nine months there working for N. W. Ayer; when I departed, I told my very kind boss that there was not enough money in the world to keep a man in Philadelphia. So this day I decided that even the steel-mill town of Pottsville would be an improvement, though it meant spending three or four hours on a whistle-stop train.

At the Pottsville station I got a cab to Unger's house, which I found filled up to the eaves with old books.

After two or three hours of rooting, I was covered with coal dust even deeper than is usual in New York bookstores. I asked if I might wash, and Unger took me upstairs. Passing through the bedroom, I stumbled over a small stack of pamphlets, and one that I noticed was a paper-bound copy of Joel Palmer's *Journal of Travels over the Rocky Mountains,* Cincinnati, 1847. I was very curious to see what Unger knew about this, so I tucked it under my elbow as I was drying my hands and then took it down to him.

"How about this?" I asked.

"Oh, that. Give me a quarter."

As I was finally making out my check for what I had decided to buy, I said, "Mr. Unger, I hear you have quite a wonderful collection of Franklin imprints. Might I see them?" I had no intention of buying any, but you know what I think about the opportunity to see and handle rarities.

Unger said very earnestly, "Everitt, I know more about Franklin imprints than practically anybody in the world, so you can't expect to buy any from me cheap."

I said I still wanted to see them, and he went on boasting about how much he knew as he led me to the safe.

One item that practically thrust itself in my face was a little pamphlet, issued with no title page, concerning the Pennsylvania, Delaware, and Maryland boundaries. In the front of this copy was a little folding map. I had recently been running through Campbell's bibliography of Franklin imprints, which noted that this pamphlet with the map was excessively rare.

"Would you sell me this?"

"I told you I know all about Franklin imprints; you can't

expect any deal here. I doubt if you could buy any of my Franklin stuff."

"All right, all right," I said. "I know that, but how much for this pamphlet?"

"Thirty dollars," said Unger, somewhat truculently.

I wrote out a second check.

As soon as I could make my escape from the state of Pennsylvania, I went with the pamphlet to George Smith.

"Oh, I've got too much stock," he said, in a tone of surfeit. "I'm only buying at auction. If you put it in a sale, I'll buy it up to seventeen hundred and fifty."

This was the way in which George's word was better than his check. I could calculate neatly enough for any banker that my take on that pamphlet would be $1750, less 15 per cent to the auctioneer.

My Palmer was at that time the only known copy in the original printed wrapper, and I got a corresponding price, though not from George.

George apparently liked a feeling of majesty about the way he paid his bills. He once owed me six hundred dollars at a time when I was very much in need of it. I went to him and said, "George, you've owed me six hundred dollars for three months."

"Sure, and I'll probably owe it to you for three more."

I looked him in the eye: "George, I need that money."

"You mean you really need it?"

I went on looking at him.

"Hey, Louis, give Everitt a check for six hundred dollars."

George's memory never betrayed him, but his vanity was stronger still. After all the big sales a number of us used to congregate at the Hotel Plaza for a few drinks. George was always a little delayed because he could not walk the three blocks from the gallery to the Plaza, but had to travel in fitting style in his Rolls-Royce.

While we were waiting for him, some wag said, "Charlie, think up a good title of some piece of rare Americana that never existed."

I devised a beauty; I wish I could remember what it was. After George's glass had been filled, I leaned over and said, "George, I think I made a mistake today. I had a copy of this thing, and I never heard of another. I let it go for five hundred, and I bet I gave it away."

George lowered the water line a little. "That? Hell, I've had two, and sold them for two hundred apiece."

"George," I said, "two bottles of Mumm's Extra Dry from you, please!"

Booksellers are constantly accused, usually with justice, of being bad businessmen. Or perhaps not with so much justice. The only occasion I ever knew when a bookseller looked up a reference offered by a customer was once when a very charming lady from Laurel, Mississippi, came in and ordered seven or eight hundred dollars' worth of books from me. She asked to have them sent. As she was leaving the shop, she said, "Oh, perhaps you'd like a reference. Just ask at Tiffany's."

Not knowing how to go about this, I went over in person to see the credit manager, who kept me waiting in line for over an hour. Finally my turn came and he said, "What can I do for you?"

I said I would like to inquire about this lady's credit.

"I don't know what your damn business is, but give it to her."

That was the end of my credit investigations.

Incidentally, Adolph Stager and I sold some $300,000 worth

of books on trust in the course of our career together, and our total losses were $32.

Here is a story proving nothing except that booksellers sometimes enjoy a little horseplay.

Somewhere Lindley Eberstadt bought the Wickersham collection of material relating to Alaska. Wickersham was the author of the standard bibliography of Alaska, and Lindley found his private library.

When he brought it in, it contained anthropology stuff that didn't interest the Eberstadts at all, but I liked the look of it. I, on the other hand, had a rare California pamphlet and no immediate customer in view. So I wandered over to swap. Ed Eberstadt said he would give me the anthropology material for the pamphlet and twenty-five dollars.

After we had argued for two or three hours, we compromised on the anthropology plus fifty dollars for the pamphlet.

In sorting out the anthropological material, I made two piles: the stuff I could use and the stuff I refused to carry away. Ed Eberstadt said all or nothing. I said, "Look here, I'm not going to pay a truck man five dollars to haul this junk."

This argument also was compromised by my leaving the junk behind.

Then Lindley Eberstadt had a stroke of genius. "Send the trash over to that cheap-book auctioneer on the East Side, to sell on commission."

No sooner said than done.

Next day I was at Eberstadts for my afternoon's arguing when the phone rang. Ed Eberstadt answered it.

"It's the auctioneer," he reported. "Says he doesn't like to sell this minor stuff on commission; he wants to buy it."

He turned back to the phone: "How much can you give us for it? . . . A hundred and a quarter? Just a minute; I don't know anything about this. I'll have to speak to my son, who bought the material."

He put a firm hand over the mouthpiece. "The damned fool wants to pay us a hundred and twenty-five bucks for that junk; now watch!"

"Well, I've just talked to my son, and he feels he really ought to get at least two hundred for material of this caliber." Ed made a face, and evidently successfully muffled the noise of his chuckles.

"A hundred and fifty? Is that really the very best you can do? Just a minute, I'll have to ask my son's opinion.

"Well, we're most reluctant to let such a collection go at a price like this, but I suppose if it's all you can afford, we'll have to meet you."

Ed had been kidding me about my ignorance of anthropology, so I checked through the list and made a rough calculation that nearly the whole lot could have been bought from the publishers, who still had the things in print, for $19.75. We all laughed our heads off until the evening after the sale. Then I added up the figures from a price catalogue, which totaled $280. Lindley's description of the gallery as a cheap-book place was true only in a very restricted way.

This reminds me that for some reason Tracy McGregor wanted a copy of a little book of lectures by President Gildersleeve of Johns Hopkins. I advertised for it until I was blue in the face, and finally some helpful soul sent in a quotation of twenty-five dollars. I forwarded it to McGregor with a notation: "This is ridiculous."

When he wanted something, he never stopped to argue. He just sent a check.

A bibliographer friend of mine happened to see the item and the bill on McGregor's desk, and wrote me a post card: "Watch your step, Charlie. The Gildersleeve book is in print with the Johns Hopkins University Press, at $1.00 less 30 per cent."

So twenty-four dollars went back by return mail to McGregor. After the number of times I have told other people to read the U. S. Catalogue, perhaps that is a cheap price for me to pay to learn that I had better do it, too.

2. *A Bookseller's Tools*

BOOKSELLERS and would-be booksellers are usually much excited to know what bibliographies and reference tools they ought to have. The problem is rather more puzzling to them because nearly every bookseller somehow accumulates several shelves of so-called reference books. The last time I called on Lathrop Harper, I noticed that if he had one auction catalogue, he had five thousand, along with at least five hundred volumes of bibliography.

I am morally certain that he never looks at so much as one of these, because he already has all the real information in his head. My own collection numbers less than fifty volumes, and in any one year I probably do not look inside more than five.

American Book Prices Current, for example, until Edward Lazare took over the editorship, was a sort of glorified pin-the-tail-on-the-donkey. You would find apparently identical copies of the same book selling in one sale for thirty dollars, and at another sale for three hundred, and not a word of explanation. Unless you were actually at the sale or had handled the particular copies in question or at least knew whether the sale had been rigged, the only dependable figure in the book was the date.

For example, if you hunt back through ABPC, you will hit on a copy of Josiah Priest's *Antiquities* of North America that sold for $45. If you were really gullible, you might even conclude that only one copy of Priest had ever been sold at auction. It is a reliable $1.50 book that you can find a good deal more often than at will: the simple truth is that nothing under five dollars gets listed in auction records for want of space.

The $45 Priest is explained by the fact that a very shrewd buying agent for a large library had a card catalogue of everything this library owned. He managed to accumulate three or four hundred items not in the card catalogue (most of them because they were too common); then he held an auction.

Morse, one of the great New York auctioneers, once told me that all he asked was three bidders: one live one and two posts. He did not conduct this particular sale, but it doesn't matter.

In the course of my career I have owned seven sets of Joseph Sabin's *Dictionary of Books Relating to America.* It takes up a lot of room and costs a lot of money; and the only real use I have ever found for this famous reference set is in the power it has given me of noting smugly in my catalogues, "Not in Sabin," and charging five dollars for fifty-cent truck.

Occasionally one may vary this by saying, "Sabin No. — " As only five hundred sets of Sabin were printed, this has the merit of mystifying the ordinary buyer.

Incidentally, anyone who honestly wants to use Sabin should get it in the microphotographed Readex version, which occupies about three inches of shelf-space.

The two reference books I use almost daily are those most people have quite forgotten about. The first is Larned's *Literature of American History;* this is invaluable to any bookseller because it lists the references by period, with an appraisal by some eminent scholar after each title.

The Pierre Margry Papers are a famous collection of documents relating to the discovery and settlement of the Mississippi Valley, published in six paper-covered volumes in 1879–1888. A set would always bring seventy-five dollars when you could find one.

We had an inquiry for a set, and as I was about to answer the letter, Harry Alpern brought over our copy of Larned, opened to the entry for Margry. It was noted that in order to finance the publication of the papers, the Library of Congress had agreed to take five hundred sets.

Harry quietly sat down and sent a post card to the Government Printing Office: "Please send two sets Margry Papers."

The sets duly arrived, with a statement that my deposit account at the GPO had been charged $4.80 per set postpaid.

A little later we quietly ordered two more sets.

When our haul had reached eight, the final shipment included a circular announcing that the price of the Margry Papers had been revised to $45.00. Once this tenfold price rise had made the book available to the ordinary bookseller, of course the whole stock was gone in no time.

Just about then, too, the GPO reported as out of print Volumes I and III of Phillips's *List of Atlases of the World,* an invaluable reference tool. Knowing the ways of the Government Printing Office, I got a friend in Washington to investigate. He reported that there were 1008 complete sets in such and such a room. For a year or two thereafter I kept myself well supplied with Phillips, always notifying the GPO where to find them.

Literature of American History came out around 1906 and has never been revised, although the WPA collected enough material to quadruple its size. The original undertaking was financed by a Canadian named George Iles, who lived at the Park Avenue Hotel in New York. He wrote an amazingly good book called *Flame, Electricity and the Camera;* but he was really more famous among all the booksellers in New York who had ten-cent counters.

As a matter of fact, Iles, like DeWitt Miller, spent a fortune in time and thoughtfulness on the ten-cent counters. He had a keen eye and a great memory, and he had friends all over the continent who were writing books on a variety of subjects. He used to distribute all his loot from the ten-cent counters around where it would do the most good.

Iles once told me about a visit he had from S. S. McClure, the publishing genius. McClure, with no money and no prospects, was just about to launch *McClure's Magazine,* which was soon to make "muckraking" a household word. During this visit McClure was passing the hat to raise capital. Iles chipped in. He felt this entitled him to ask, "Sam, why are you wearing that Prince Albert coat?"

McClure lifted up his coattails. "Because I've got a hole in the seat of my pants."

After *McClure's Magazine* had become an established success, McClure serialized in it his autobiography, which Willa Cather helped him with. It was a success story, of course, but McClure's whole life was a dizzy series of ups and downs. As a matter of fact, he survived into the late 1940's (which would have amazed 98 per cent of the people who had known of him in his great days), and was not even able to make his own living.

At all events, the autobiography was advertised with placards on every wall and in every bus: "I came to New York with twenty-five cents."

I saw one along Fourth Avenue on which somebody had neatly inscribed: "I bet he wishes he had it now!"

George Iles was once at a party given by Henry E. Huntington, at which some of Huntington's treasures were shown.

Mr. Huntington was displaying a first edition of *Pilgrim's Progress,* and Mr. Iles observed, "I hear you're giving away souvenirs today. I'd love to have that one."

Iles told me, "They watched me like a hawk the rest of the afternoon."

The other reference book that I use all the time was issued in 1905 by the American Historical Association: Griffith's *Publications of American Historical Societies.* This is a veritable gold mine of information about biographical monographs and the like.

I remember once I had a telephone call from the vice-president of a bank who said he was very anxious indeed to find some biography of his great-grandfather, Hugh Williamson, the author of a history of North Carolina. In Griffith I learned that the New York Historical Society had published a pamphlet about Williamson early in the nineteenth century, and I soon dug out three copies from among the 25,000 odd pamphlets in my stock. I took one copy, spent fifty cents at Fridenberg's for a portrait, and had MacDonald put on a ten-dollar red morocco binding. Then I sent the finished product to the banker with a bill for fifty dollars. He paid, and sent me an effusive note with his check. Two years later he telephoned again, and I braced myself in case he should have found out just how scarce his grandfather's biography really was. After all, I *had* put on a pretty binding.

What he said was, "Mr. Everitt, does lightning ever strike twice in the same place? Could you possibly find me another copy of that biography?"

Rapidly calculating how long it would take me to go through my own stock, I said, "Well, if you have quite a good deal of patience, I hope I may be able to find you another in four or five months."

I did.

Another reference tool that I have reason to remember vividly, although I don't look at it very often, is Bradford's *Bibliographer's Manual of American History,* which is actually just a list of state, county, and town histories, issued (and probably compiled, I suspect) by Stan V. Henkels, the Philadelphia book auctioneer. Bradford is in five quarto volumes. It was published at fifteen dollars, in an edition strictly limited to five hundred sets.

I bought twenty-five sets from Stan Henkels at fifteen dollars less discount, sold them, and bought and sold another twenty-five sets. Then I happened to be in Philadelphia, and he said, "Don't you want to buy fifty sets at three-fifty a set?"

I said, "Sure, send them over."

I catalogued these at a reduced price and promptly sold them all. Some weeks later I was down there again, and Henkels asked if I did not want to buy all that was left of the original five hundred sets at $2.50 a set. Having sold a hundred sets with very little difficulty myself, I thought I could probably get rid of what few remained.

Within a few days a truck pulled up to my 34th Street store, and dumped off cartons containing 410 sets. There were 2050 volumes, all wrapped in newspaper, quite unmarked in any way. It took two of my men three weeks to sort out the volumes. They have all disappeared, as they well deserved to, since this is still the only inclusive bibliography of American local history.

Henkels, one of the great figures in American book auctioneering, was an unreconstructed Confederate. An appeal to his Southern patriotism was the only thing that could unsettle his judgment.

Horace Hayden, librarian of the Wyoming Valley Historical Society at Wilkes-Barre, Pennsylvania, was the author of *Virginia Genealogies,* one of the most famous volumes in its field. He sent me a note saying, "I'm getting pretty old, and I think I have too many books. Do you want to buy them?"

I went down and offered him $3500. He said he would let me know. He did: he had had a letter from Stan Henkels. Henkels wrote: "Don't let that damned Yankee Charlie Everitt rob you. Send the books down here, and I'll get you twice whatever he offers."

The next time I saw Dr. Hayden at Wilkes-Barre was some months after he had received a check from Stan Henkels for $2200. I said, "This business of Southern gentlemen's sticking together is pretty expensive, isn't it?"

Said Dr. Hayden: "Everitt, don't you think you should let sleeping dogs lie?"

Unfortunately in his last years Stan Henkels was annoyed with me. I wrote something that got printed about the pamphlets I bought in one of his sales for $45 and sold for $1400. My last communication from him was a note: "Charlie, you're a damned liar." For once in my life I was not, but there was no answer to be made.

Among the purchases I made from Henkels's auction galleries were some volumes of Texas newspapers. I sent a man down there, telling him to buy the stuff if he could get it for $250.

He came back with the loot, and remarked, "Everitt, you don't know anything about newspapers. Here." Handing me a bill for $14, he collected $1.40 commission.

I was just in the act of collating the papers when Tom Streeter came in. As he was looking over my shoulder, a volume fell open to a broadside from the period of Texas independence.

"How much?" said Streeter, eagerly.

"Oh, a hundred and fifty."

Three or four pages further on, another broadside.

"How much?"

"A hundred and fifty."

A few pages further on, the rarest Texas broadside in the world. The bottom had been torn off. It was one of Stephen Austin's pronouncements, no copy of which had ever been seen before.

"How much for that, Charlie?"

"With my compliments, Tom; you'll never complete it."

The next time I was in London I had a letter from Streeter saying: "Here are the last seven lines of that broadside; I found them in a Missouri newspaper. See what you can do with it." The text of the broadside had been reprinted, and he had copied off the last part for me.

I took the defective broadside and the missing text to Zaehnsdorf's world-famous bindery and asked what they could do about it.

"This will cost you a lot of money," said Ernest Zaehnsdorf.

"I didn't ask about that; I asked what you could do," I said, and departed for Scotland.

When I got back, they had completed the broadside so perfectly that only a magnifying glass would tell where the original stopped and the copy began. They had lettered in the type by hand.

"This is beautiful," I said. "What will it cost?"

"Well, it took a man seven days to do it. You can give me seven pounds."

This is one occasion when the discovery of a unique item has not lured out any further copies. Tom Streeter's, cobbled as it is, remains alone.

In trying to keep this book as pure as Ivory soap claims to be, I've looked over a good many volumes about bookselling and book collecting. The only one that struck me as completely truthful is the *Memoirs of the Life of Mr. James Lackington,* a great London bookseller, who, like me, was brought up a devout Methodist. In middle life, after telling tales of book transactions that he felt were less than perfectly honest, he recanted and became an agnostic. Later on, he apparently began to worry about the future, returned to Methodism, and wrote another pious Methodist book. I have not followed him that far.

Of all the millions of words that have been written about bookselling and rare books, most are damn nonsense. The whole thing is really nothing but a battle of wits.

One bookselling book, Tommy Spencer's *Forty Years in My Bookshop,* is an example of most of its kind, and I don't think too much of it. Possibly I am prejudiced. On my first trip to London I had a number of invitations from Mr. Spencer to come in. When I finally went, I saw a bunch of junk over in one corner, and to save my face, I picked out two or three things that I thought were worth carting away.

"Oh, those books are married," said Spencer. (This is an English trade term for what we here call a "tie-in" sale – you buy all the books or none.)

I had made up my mind to spend probably five quid on brother Spencer, so I priced the married lot.

"You can have those for a hundred quid."

"Good-by. I'll be seeing you soon." And off I went.

It happened that Erhard Weyhe of New York, the world's greatest dealer in art books, was staying at the same hotel where I was. He spoke to me that evening. "Do you want to buy anything from Spencer?"

"Oh, he has some junk that I'd be willing to have."

"Well, come along with me. I'm going to spend two or three thousand pounds down there tonight, and he'll sell you what you want at any price or no price to get you out of the place."

So down we went. The fat Mr. Spencer kept shifting uneasily in his chair, and did not seem at all glad to see me. "Well, uh, Mr. Everitt, what will you give me for that lot of Americana?"

"Well, I was thinking of ten quid."

"Take them away," said Spencer with a sweep of the arm and a great sigh of relief.

The only comparable book to Spencer's that I can think of in this country is Dr. Abraham S. W. Rosenbach's *Books and Bidders.*

Some other attempts have been made along the same line, but so far as I know, no other book equals these two.

If you think gooey writing is a thing of the past, let me

quote to you from the *Antiquarian Bookman* of June 3, 1950. "We want bookshops pleasant to enter into, catalogues beguiling to order out of, libraries treasure-houses of pleasure, not mausoleums, collectors' meetings as merry and many as possible." If I ever go into this dream bookshop, I think it will take two bottles of Mothersill's Remedy and two quarts of Old Taylor before I feel comfortable again. As to the kind of libraries described, to say nothing of the collectors' meetings, thank God, they don't exist.

"But," the editor continues, "there are no 'trade secrets.' We do pay off on knowledge, but this is available to all who will take the trouble to seek it out."

I know of no fifty-six words that contain so much misinformation about bookselling. If you had all, or even half, the trade secrets (by which I mean information not listed in any bibliography) in the heads of Lathrop Harper, Edward Eberstadt, Mike Walsh, Ernest Wessen, Sam Dauber, Leon Kashnor, Mark Cohen, Charlie Harris, and a few others like them, you could — as I have said before this — make a very handsome living out of rare books without a dollar of capital or a single volume of bibliography.

As you may have concluded from my letter-carrier friend's experience with Beck's *Illinois Gazetteer*, on the other hand, bibliographies and reference books are not worth a damn anyway unless you know how to use them.

One of the most solemn bookselling organizations I know of will never sell an old book until they have searched all their own catalogues and all the other catalogues and price lists in their extensive reference library. They are very much afraid of giving away something for nothing. But at the same time there has to be some end to their pains. Since the various volumes of *American Book Prices Current* do not bother with items that auctioned below five dollars, these good people have established a working rule that any book they cannot find must be worth about $3.50.

On one occasion I bought some Mexican pamphlets concerning California. There were three items that they had not been able to find in the reference books. "We'll call you up when we've priced these," their man said.

After a while he did so, and gave me the not unexpected news that the price of each was $3.50 less 10 per cent.

Since all I said was, "All right, send them over," I hope I showed no excitement. But the parcel post took four days, and I got a little uneasy.

All was well, however, when they arrived, and I personally delivered them to a Western specialist who paid me nine hundred dollars for two of them.

I don't know exactly how I have developed a feel for telling when such unprepossessing-looking junk is worthless and when it is priceless. For one thing, although I can only pick out about six words of Spanish, I have a sharp eye for such names as California, Oregon, and Texas, no matter how baffling the words that surround them. When I see these words in a Mexican publication between 1830 and 1848, the chances are that the thing is not recorded, not because it is too cheap to bother with, but because it is unique.

Once when I came back from a London trip, my partner Stager said smugly, "Dauber & Pine had a cattle-trade map catalogued for seven-fifty. So I bought it, and sold it for fifty dollars."

"Adolph," I said, "Dauber & Pine were pretty stupid, but

you were a lot stupider." The map had been issued in the 1880's by one of the Western railroads, and only three copies had ever been heard of.

In those days I lived down near Dauber & Pine's and used to drop in almost every night. Sam Dauber buttonholed me. "I had two copies of that cattle map, Charlie," he said, "but Adolph tried to beat me down to five dollars, so I didn't tell him. Would you like the other copy?"

"Sure, I'll give you seven-fifty with no argument at all," I said.

I turned mine over for $350. When the buyer's estate was sold up not so very long afterward, the map brought $475.

In other words, it's imagination, not bibliography, that makes money.

Sometimes I think that the followers of A. Edward Newton, Merle Johnson, and Barton Currie should all go to a psychiatrist; then I wonder whether psychiatrists can do any good to sheep.

One of the most famous "tools" for first edition collectors is Merle Johnson's *American First Editions.* When Johnson was putting the book together, he said to me, "Charlie, this is just a game, like checkers. If I can persuade a man that one edition of a book is worth five dollars, and another edition is worth three hundred, then I can sell him the three-hundred-dollar one."

He and I had a long argument over the true first edition of Richard Henry Dana, Jr.'s *Two Years Before the Mast.* Harper & Brothers put out one edition in black cloth and another, cheaper, in their "school library." I kept telling Johnson I had never heard of a publisher's putting out a cheap reprint before the original edition. During this argument I sold a very nice copy in black cloth to a collector from Pittsburgh for a hundred dollars. Johnson could not see the force of my argument, as in his collector's bible he insisted that the "school library" edition was the first. My Pittsburgh collector, reading Johnson, declared I had robbed him. I told him that books were always sold on the basis of the best knowledge at the time when they were sold. He was not satisfied.

I said I would be glad to give him $150 for the book. He said all bibliographers and booksellers were a pack of scoundrels, and he was going to sell his collection and never buy another book. At the sale the *Two Years Before the Mast* that he complained about brought $275. For a while after the issue of Johnson's bibliography the "school library" edition sold for as much as $1200.

Johnson's book has since undergone several revisions at the hands of Jacob Blanck, and is now as accurate as any reference book can be. Let me remark, parenthetically that it calls the black cloth *Two Years Before the Mast* the true first edition.

Apropos of books about book collecting, one of the greatest living bibliographers is Mr. R. W. G. Vail. I can hardly ever remember catching him in a mistake, but I treasure as a sublime understatement the following note in his *The Literature of Book Collecting:* "Currie, Barton Wood, Fishers of Books . . . Pleasantly written, not always accurate . . . A melancholy souvenir of frenzied collecting at top-notch prices before the crash."

One of the best and most down-to-earth books about books I know is Leon Vincent's *Life of DeWitt Miller.*

Miller was among my favorite book collectors. He made a good living as a Chautauqua lecturer. When he was not on the platform, he was usually infesting some old bookstore. He could be sure of a warm welcome in every shop in the country. He used to carry a green cloth lawyer's bag three feet long, and seldom left a bookstore without filling it to the top.

You could never tell what he was going to buy; it might be anything in the whole field of literature, biography, or history. Eight out of every ten books he bought he was likely to inscribe and send off to friends.

(Incidentally, he took a fiendish delight in buying at secondhand stores copies he had autographed and sending them back to the original recipients.)

Miller had the best accidental collection of great rarities I ever knew of. He cared nothing about rarities as such; his method was to go into a bookstore, pull a bagful of volumes off the shelves, never looking at the prices, and say, "How much?"

In the small-town shops where he usually went, the dealers were just as innocent about five-hundred-dollar books as he was. So he accumulated an incredible collection without anyone's being the wiser, least of all himself.

His conscious ambition was to accumulate a perfect working library, and in this he succeeded admirably. At the time of his death he had many thousands of volumes.

He left this library to a small school in Maryland, along with money to brace up a building to house it. The trustees after a few years called in an auctioneer, who picked out about three hundred volumes from the thousands of books. He must have been stunned by the quantity, because he overlooked at least ten times as many rarities as he took.

Then, within a few years, the trustees showed that their library training had not been wasted: they decided that the building was overcrowded, and sold all the books to a bookshop I know for a few dollars above the freight charges.

The owners of that bookshop not only lived on this collection for a decade, but they are still selling items from it.

The first rule of sound practice for any collector, and indeed any dealer, is to establish a firm connection with someone he can trust, and not keep shopping around in search of an extra dollar. (You may remember that Mr. Ford thought it cheaper to pay me fifteen dollars for something than to keep hunting until he could buy it for ten dollars.) Quite aside from the time you waste, dealing with a friend often shows a better dollar balance.

I once had a letter from a real-estate man in Virginia inquiring about a manuscript he had. He said he did not know what it was, and would like it appraised or perhaps sold. I wrote him to send it on, and to be sure to ship it express, insured. This is the easiest and quietest way of finding out how high an owner himself values his property. The manuscript arrived, insured for twenty-five dollars. When I looked it over, I found that it was the original manuscript of Gookin's *Indians of New England.*

First I went to the oracle, Mr. Eames, to learn if the manuscript had ever been printed. He soon told me that it had been printed in the *Transactions* of the American Antiquarian Society, and, furthermore, that this identical manuscript had served the printer as copy.

I wrote the owner that I did not know what the manuscript was really worth, but that I could get him fifteen hundred dollars immediately, or three thousand if he were not in a great hurry.

He wired that he was coming to town next day. His first

and practically only act was to claim his manuscript and scoot out of the store.

I filled in by the grapevine what happened afterward. He took the manuscript to the largest auction gallery in the country, whose Americana expert assured him I was robbing him. He said the manuscript would bring five thousand at the very least. When the precious manuscript came up at auction, a colleague of mine bought it for four hundred dollars.

I sent a postcard to the former owner: "Your not liking my face was pretty expensive."

For a person who has made much of his living through six decades by reading booksellers' catalogues, I find myself peculiarly apt to be enraged by them. The other day I was reading a catalogue in which the word "scarce" appeared forty-seven times and the word "rare" eleven times. Out of the fifty-eight, none was rare; one of the "rare" ones was, as a matter of fact, rather scarce.

Somehow I don't mind this quite so much when the bookseller privately knows better. For instance, I once stopped at Charles Chadenat's famous bookshop in Paris. Chadenat welcomed me with considerable ceremony. I found he had a rope across the door of his rare-book room.

"America has driven down the value of the franc, and I don't want to sell any rarities until the franc has risen again," he explained. "However, you and Mr. Harper have been good customers of mine for years, and if you can come back tomorrow, I will be glad to show you any Western Americana I may have." When I came back, he produced, with an air of religious awe, a French volume about the California gold rush. The word "rare" seemed to take on new meaning as he explained and gesticulated. It was really a gesture of international good will to allow such a gem to pass from his hands to mine. Furthermore, it was as fresh as the day it came from the bindery.

My experience is that books as clean as this have usually been protected by having other copies on each side of them. I said, "That's fine, Monsieur Chadenat. I'll be glad to take ten copies."

He flushed with mortification. "But I only have eight."

By the way, my own rule-of-thumb definition of a scarce book is one that you have to spend two or three years hunting for; of a rare book, one that you can't find in ten or twenty years.

PART IV

C.P.E.

EVERYONE knows that the cobbler's children have no shoes. By the same token, very few booksellers read. If I have any eccentricity as a bookseller, I suppose it is my habit of reading my wares. This in turn I got from my mother, who was a country schoolteacher in Andover, New Jersey. There have been many lists of books that influenced American thought, but sixty-five years ago practically none of these lists were available in the country. Instead, my mother used to read aloud at least three nights a week. When I was a boy, the family library consisted of a Bible, a set of Josephus, and a copy of E. P. Roe's *Barriers Burned Away,* a novel about the Chicago fire. To this day, I know nothing more about the Chicago fire.

The library kept pace with me in its growth. The additions included John Habberton's *Helen's Babies,* Harriet Beecher Stowe's *Old Town Folks,* a volume of California humor called *Phoenixiana,* and another of Mrs. Stowe's novels, which impressed me at the time more than any of the others, *Dred.* I still think it a better story than *Uncle Tom's Cabin.*

Between feeding three farmhands, making butter, and milking cows when some of our men were drunk, my mother spent four months reading *Vanity Fair* aloud. My only surviving impression of this is that Becky Sharp is one of the most vicious characters in fiction.

When I was twelve years old, I was presented with a copy of *The Last of the Mohicans.* I was lucky enough to find a place on the roof where my father could not see me; so when I was supposed to be chopping kindling for the next day, I would be reading about Natty Bumppo.

When my own children came along, I assumed that they would enjoy the Leatherstocking Tales, so I presented each one with a set. None of them could read Cooper at all.

So I tried to reread those stodgy volumes, and discovered that my children were dead right.

So many years ago that I have quite lost count, I had an open bookshop across the street from Wanamaker's. A woman I knew slightly came in one day, and asked if I had ever heard of Rudyard Kipling.

"Who is Rudyard Kipling?" I asked, or words to that effect.

She gave me a copy of John Lovell's edition of *Barrack Room Ballads.* I read it.

Of course you know how youngsters (I was in my twenties) are carried away by enthusiasm for a book. I was carried away by that one, and the odd thing is I have never changed my mind. I thought then, and I think now, that Rudyard Kipling was the greatest writer of my generation. I may not live to see his reputation back where it belongs, but it will come back.

I have always had the run of Frank Doubleday's publishing offices; I worked for him once, and my brother was his partner. Doubleday was noted for his enormous wastebasket, which stood up higher than his desk. One day I was in his office, and noticed some galley proofs just within my reach in his wastebasket.

"What are those, Effendi?" I asked.

"Oh, those are the galleys of *Kim*. We've gone into pages, and we don't need the galleys."

I fished the proofs out. There seemed to be two or three hundred corrections in Kipling's hand.

"Look here, Effendi," I said, "fifty-fifty on what I get for these."

The great Kipling collector of that time was a man named Williamson. He got a bargain when he paid me $750 for the galleys.

As Kipling became better known, copyright protection on his works grew important. Until recently it was necessary in such cases, under American copyright law, to make separate printings. Two copies had to go to the Library of Congress, and two copies had to be billed to some dealer. I remember as if it were yesterday the time when Doubleday, my brother Sam, and Kipling stood by the press while the special copyright printing of *The White Man's Burden* came off. The edition was ten copies, and then the type was destroyed.

I was the dealer involved. Two copies of the poem were billed to me at $1.50 less 40 per cent, ninety cents each.

Kipling inscribed a copy to J. L. Thompson, Doubleday's business manager. I don't ever expect to know what happened to the other three copies.

With what I hope is less than my usual imagination, I sold my two copies to collectors at fifty dollars apiece. Quite a while later I sold the Thompson copy to Mr. Ellis A. Ballard, the great Philadelphia collector, for fifteen hundred dollars. When Kipling collectors utterly vanished, the Ballard collection was sold at the American Art Association Galleries for about 10 per cent of its appraised value. Still, one consolation was that *The White Man's Burden,* the high spot of the sale, brought five hundred dollars.

During the Kipling boom, without question the outstanding authority on Kipling was Travers Brown, a bookseller with a wonderful knowledge of first editions; he was also a friend of mine, a diabetic, and perfectly irresponsible. He used to play bridge at my house all the time, lose steadily, and leave me to pay his losses. He also bought, or at least picked out and removed, books from my shop.

One day he asked me down for a drink. His diabetes had been getting worse. "Charlie," he said, "I'm going to commit suicide tomorrow. Have your man Harry come down to the store and pick out anything he wants so as to settle our account."

"It's all right with me, Travers," I said. "I haven't the slightest idea what you owe me anyway." And I departed for New Hampshire.

My man Friday, Harry Alpern, went down as instructed and picked out some books, including the Montdale and Livingston bibliographies of Kipling. They contained not hundreds but thousands of additional notes by Brown. I gave the matter no further thought until I got back from New Hampshire. Then I discovered that Harry, being afraid I would worry, had not notified me that Mr. Brown had jumped off a boat.

My connections with the firm of Doubleday kept me well supplied with Kipling material for a good many years. One item that passed through my hands rather embarrassed me. While I was away, John Phillips, who had been Doubleday's editor, and also a partner in the firm of McClure, Phillips, came into the store with some books because he was moving to Goshen, New York. Harry Alpern quite innocently and unsuspectingly gave him a hundred dollars for the lot.

On my return I discovered that the books included Mark Twain's privately printed *What Is Man?* and two chapters of the original manuscript of *Stalky & Co.* Everybody's intentions had been of the best; I could not go back on Harry; and Phillips did not need the money, so we left it at that. I sold the Mark Twain for a hundred and fifty dollars, and sat back to wait with the Kipling.

My phone rang, and a voice said, "I'm Stewart, from Halifax, Nova Scotia. Sam Dauber tells me you have some unusual Kipling material. Could you come down to the Ritz-Carlton and show it to me?"

At the Ritz-Carlton I found a man on two crutches, who introduced himself and apologized for not being able to call at my store. In his room he had two satchels, one on each side of his chair.

First I showed him several of my scarce copyright printings. He looked each one over, said, "I have that," and reached for the next.

Then I showed him a little book of recitations, containing Kipling's first American appearance in print.

"What's this worth?" he asked.

I said, "Ten cents, and I want fifty dollars for it."

Mr. Stewart reached down into the left satchel and handed me a fifty-dollar bill.

"Now," he went on, "I see you have some manuscript of *Stalky & Co.*" He looked at the pages for a moment, and went on, "I understand from Mr. Dauber that you want a thousand dollars for this."

I said yes.

He reached down into the right-hand satchel and handed me twenty Canadian fifty-dollar bills.

"Wait a minute," he said, "the Canadian exchange is against us." And he reached into the left-hand satchel and gave me an American fifty-dollar bill.

"Now," I said, "Mr. Stewart, would you have any objection to telling me what the hell this is all about? I know you are a friend of Kipling's, and that's all I do know."

"Well, I have a paper business up in Halifax that makes me a few dollars, and every once in so often I like to go on a binge. Most of the time I won't answer letters, look at catalogues, pay any attention to booksellers' quotations, or anything else. Then I break out. I happen to have the feeling that Kipling is the most important man in my lifetime, or your lifetime, and I'd like to get together the best Kipling collection there is. We have a little university up in Halifax, doesn't amount to much, but anyway I mean to give this collection to the university. Probably not a son of a bitch in the world will ever look at it, but if it provides any inspiration to just one man, that's all I need."

After Travers Brown's suicide, I offered his annotated Kipling bibliographies to Mr. Stewart for $500. Mr. Stewart did not feel they were worth more than $250, so I hung on to them. If he wants them today for $50, they are his.

(By the way, *The White Man's Burden* was the last copyright printing of which exact records were kept. No bibliographer will ever know how many copies were printed of the innumerable subsequent copyright issues. The boys in Doubleday's office suddenly discovered there was a good thing to be made out of these, and for some time special Kipling copyright printings could be bought, at steadily rising prices.)

* * *

The year I was pinch-hitting for J. L. Thompson, the sales manager for Doubleday, Page & Co., the firm published a novel by Alfred Ollivant called *Bob, Son of Battle*. All our readers and all our editors agreed that it was the best dog story ever written.

By advertising extensively and trying to spread our own personal enthusiasm, we managed (with some difficulty) to sell a few hundred copies.

One day Frank Doubleday was in my office, feeling very doleful about our pet book.

"Charlie, I just can't understand it. Here's a book written by a man in a wheel chair, which everybody around here insists is the best dog story ever put on paper. We have a fistful of reviews that say the same thing. We spend hundreds of dollars trying to tell the public about it. And then what? Our salesmen come back and say they can't get it onto the bookseller's shelves with a sledge hammer. Are you crazy?"

"Effendi," I said, "you go back to your office and write down what you've just been telling me. Let me make an ad out of *that*."

The next issue of the *World's Work* (which Doubleday owned) contained a full-page ad headed: "The Autobiography of a Novel." In the following six months we must have sold fifty thousand copies. A publisher's real problem is making people listen the first time.

Frank Doubleday had an extremely well-grounded skepticism about the merchandising abilities of American booksellers. Whenever he really wanted to sell many copies of a book, he would think up a brand-new outlet.

Bliss Perry edited for him three ten-volume sets of *Little Classics*. The sale through the bookstores was downright miserable. Finally Perry got discouraged, came to Doubleday, and said, "I don't see any future for these wretched things. If you can give me a few hundred dollars in cash, I'll be glad to sign a receipt for payment in full."

Doubleday gave him the check, and Perry put on his hat and departed.

The door had hardly slammed behind him when Frank Doubleday, true to his mistrust of the book trade, went down to see Charles Lanier, of the *Review of Reviews*. He extracted from Lanier an order for 300,000 volumes of the *Little Classics*.

In the next two or three years Lanier reordered more than once, in quantities almost equal to the original order.

Doubleday scrupulously sent royalty checks to Bliss Perry (which was not enough to keep Perry in the Doubleday stable of authors).

In 1896, my boss, Summerfield MacLean, bought a tremendous library of Anglican theology. I found myself taking an interest in it, and became something of a specialist in Anglican bibliography. While MacLean was dispersing the library, Bishop Darlington of Pittsburgh was an almost daily frequenter of the store. He could never resist a seventeenth-century book, regardless of the subject.

We supplied him with these, and he began bringing in his friends. One in particular, Reverend Stewart Crockett, came almost as often as the bishop. When he discovered that I had a smattering of Episcopalian bibliography, he used to hold most of his dealings with me.

Bishop Darlington was an eminently free-and-easy, jovial backslapper, whom I had got into the habit of treating not at all as you might expect a bishop to be treated. More or less unconsciously I extended the habit to Dr. Crockett. Apparently this was a mistake; or perhaps it wasn't. Anyway, one day as Dr. Crockett was leaving the store, he turned and said, "Everitt, will you deliver a message to your wife?"

I said I would be glad to.

"You tell Mrs. Everitt that I shall be glad to preach your funeral sermon gratis."

"Will you indeed?" I said. "What are you going to say?"

"The simplest thing in the world. I'll stand up beside the coffin and just say, 'We all hope he's gone where we know he hasn't.'"

Only a few months later Crockett was robbed of this pleasure by death. I appraised his library, and of course made no charge.

In October of 1898 I left Summerfield MacLean and opened my own bookstore at 18 East 23rd Street, underneath the Scott Stamp and Coin Company. I had a few books and $303 in cash, but more shelves than books. That was the season when Kipling's *The Day's Work* came out, and I had my window full of it, along with some theological books.

After a few weeks I had a visit from the janitor of the Catherine Wolfe house at 24th Street and Madison Avenue.

Miss Wolfe had recently died, leaving her estate under the care of David Wolfe Bishop and Cortlandt Field Bishop, the latter of whom owned the American Art Association Galleries. They had sold the house to the Metropolitan Life Insurance Company, which later put up the present building on the site.

The janitor's tale was that Mr. Bishop had sent several barrels of old books downstairs with instructions to burn them, but the janitor thought he might pick up a dollar or two by speaking to me.

I went over to look at the rubbish, which proved to be

American pamphlets. "How much do you want for these?" I asked.

"Oh, give me five dollars," said the janitor.

Not unnaturally, I was uneasy. I said that I would be glad to do business if the janitor could give me a note from Mr. Bishop.

He came back with the note in about ten minutes, and I handed him fifty dollars. Part of this princely sum was to pay for his bringing the barrels over in a wheelbarrow.

One of the axioms in the rare-book trade is that the grapevine spreads word of any important new collection like wildfire. One bookseller called on me by accident the next morning; he couldn't keep his mouth shut; when I opened the store the morning after, seven booksellers were on the doorstep.

I took in two or three thousand dollars that day (none of it accounted for by Kipling or theology). As I look back now, I realize that I was a good deal stupider than the janitor who sold me the lot for fifty dollars.

Thanks to Mr. Bishop and his janitor, and in spite of my own ignorance, I accumulated quite a fair-sized bankroll for a bookseller. I was very glad of it when I got a letter from the widow of a man who had been postmaster in Harrisburg for sixty-five years.

I went down to look over his library, which was a very nice one. We agreed on a price of around twelve hundred dollars; I wrote my check and was about to leave.

"Just a minute," she said. "Let me get out that old box. My husband kept a sheet of every stamp that was issued during his sixty-five years as postmaster. Could you afford to give me five dollars for the lot?"

I looked at the contents of the box. There were about five

hundred dollars' worth, face value, of uncanceled stamps there.

"Look," I said, "I have my ticket to New York, and $205 in cash on me. I'll give you two hundred dollars, but I strongly advise you not to take it, because I think you can do much better."

"If I offer it to you for five dollars, and you offer me two hundred," she replied, "I think it would be most unethical of me not to accept." So I shelled out the two hundred dollars, and added the stamps to my take.

Back in New York I went upstairs to Scott's, and put the stamps on the desk of John Luff, who was the leading stamp authority of the time.

"John," I said, "I want you to pick out all the stamps in here that are selling at a premium, and let me have the rest to use for postage."

A couple of hours later he came down. "Here, I'll give you two thousand for these, and that will leave you about three hundred dollars' worth of stamps to stick on your envelopes."

I looked at him. "John, are you robbing me plenty?"

He looked right back. "You bet your damn life." And we closed the deal.

One of the finest libraries that has passed through my hands belonged to William H. Egle, the Pennsylvania historian. It was rich in genealogies. As I was thumbing through one volume, I came on a single sheet of paper; it was in crabbed German, but I finally figured out that it consisted of ten birth notices of members of the Bollinger family. It was printed in 1763 at Ephrata, Pennsylvania, the great seat of pre-Revolutionary German-American printing. Dr. Egle had written in the margin, "The first known genealogical record printed in America."

By this time I was a real expert, so I boldly priced the broadside at $150.

The morning after my catalogue was mailed, the librarian of one of the three largest genealogical societies in the country telephoned long distance. "Have you still got that Bollinger broadside?"

"Yes."

"Is it mine?"

"Sure."

"All right, then. Everitt, you aren't so hot. We've been advertising for years that we would pay a thousand dollars for that broadside if we could find one."

I may have lost a paper profit on the Bollinger genealogy. Another item in the same catalogue brought me a valuable and much cherished friendship. There was a book by William Byrd of Virginia, written in German and printed in Switzerland in 1737, entitled (in translation) *New Found Eden.* I have since concluded that this was certainly almost the first, and probably *the* first, attempt at real-estate promotion in Virginia and North Carolina. I was trying to work up nerve enough to tag it a hundred dollars.

Looking for moral support, I spoke to Daniel Parish, of the New York Historical Society, who used to frequent my store.

"I don't know a thing about this kind of stuff," he said, "but there's a man named Wilberforce Eames up at the Lenox Library who knows more about it than any other person living. He's a nice fellow. Why not go see him?"

So up I went with my *New Found Eden.* The Lenox Library in those days, before it became part of the New York Public Library, was in the East Seventies. Mr. Eames welcomed me in, looked over my book, and got out his copy.

When we compared them, it turned out that his copy had only one map, whereas mine had two.

"What is your price for your copy, Mr. Everitt?" he asked.

"I haven't the slightest idea. I came to you for information about it, and I'm as ignorant as a babe unborn."

I supposed that concluded the interview, and I was just getting ready to leave when Mr. Eames said, "If you would consider taking two hundred and fifty and our copy, lacking one map, we should be very delighted indeed to have your copy."

I did not dawdle very long about trading copies, and went back to the store with his copy instead of mine.

It was my good luck to have many occasions afterward for discovering that Mr. Eames was the one librarian who never made a mistake about a book. No other copy of Byrd's *New Found Eden* has ever been offered for sale (although the printing of these words will probably bring four copies to the surface).

About 1902 or 1903 John Francis (who had worked with me at Summerfield MacLean's) and I started the Everitt & Francis Company. We made some money, but not enough to satisfy two such ambitious operators, so we rented a huge store at 114 East 23rd Street. A man came in one day and said, "I'm moving. I have a bunch of old books, and if you'll pay for the express, you're welcome to them." He never gave his name, and I was not interested enough to ask.

A little while later an expressman delivered a large packing case, and demanded seventy-five cents' ransom. I happened to be out, and one of the boys paid the seventy-five cents.

When I got back, I pawed through the contents of the case. "Well," I said, "we're out only seventy-five cents anyway. Wait a minute, what's this?"

It was the paper cover to J. Q. Howard's *Life of Lincoln*, Cincinnati, 1860. Just the cover, no contents.

"Oh, a lot of those were used to stuff out the case."

"What did you do with them?"

"Put them down cellar."

"All right, take this trash down cellar, and bring them up instead."

He staggered back upstairs with a load of twenty-eight copies in original paper wrappers.

I sat down and wrote to Major William H. Lambert of Philadelphia, then the greatest Lincoln collector. "How would you like a copy of Howard's *Life of Lincoln* for ten dollars?" I asked.

He replied in crisp military fashion by endorsement on my note: "There is no such book."

So I sent him a copy.

He sent back two ten-dollar bills, with a note; "Send another copy." Herman Sauer, the wisest Lincoln scout of the time, bought five copies. He did not think it worth calling to my attention something I had not noticed, namely, that one of the copies he bought was in German. This, I learned later, he sold to Charles McLellan, of Boody, McLellan & Company, for a hundred dollars.

Colonel McLellan was a Confederate officer who spent all the latter half of his life buying books about Lincoln. John D. Rockefeller, Jr., eventually bought his collection and gave it to the Brown University library. (The last sale prices of Howard's *Lincoln* that I heard of were $250 for the German, and two copies of the English for $150 each.)

At this time Emmanuel Hertz was just launching on his interest in Lincolniana. He told me that J. Q. Howard was still alive, and still working at a job that Lincoln had given him as a reward for writing the biography, in the Library of Congress. I wrote to Mr. Howard, asking if he could tell me anything about his *Life of Lincoln.*

Two-line reply: "If you want my autograph, send me two dollars." I did not want his autograph, so I wrote to John Hay, Lincoln's biographer, asking what he knew.

His reply ran to two pages. The meat of it was that Howard had written the biography of Lincoln for campaign purposes, but that Lincoln had thought so poorly of it that no copies were ever distributed to the public. (I put this reply in my files, which I am sorry to say I have discovered are even more bottomless than those of the Government; or at least I don't know where Mr. Hay's letter is.)

Major Lambert, in addition to his Lincoln collection, had a fine lot of Thackeray. One day a stranger, looking rather woebegone, came into my 23rd Street store and said he had just been to a book auction and had made a mistake. He had bought a set of Mrs. Chapone's pious *Letters,* which the cataloguer said had some notes in Thackeray's hand. His enthusiasm had run away with him, and he had paid three dollars. I said all right, I would help him out of his predicament.

Next morning I came to the store rather late and found him sitting on the steps. "I know I went crazy on this, and I'm willing to lose a dollar, if you want to give me two dollars."

That far I was willing to go, so money and books changed hands.

When I looked over my purchase, I found that almost every page contained some supercilious scribble by Thackeray about the author's goody-goody sentiments. So I sent the set to Major Lambert, and asked him how he would like to pay me $250 for it.

He wrote back that the books were dirt cheap, but he had all the Thackeray junk he wanted.

Next I reassured myself by taking the set to the Scribner Book Store, where Safford, then the head of the rare-book department, said there was no mistake, this was the real thing.

Just as I was talking to Safford, Ernest Dressel North drifted in. He vanished again, and lay in wait for me outside the door.

"How much?"

"Two hundred and fifty dollars."

"All right, send me a bill."

Being broke, as was my custom, I said I was willing to go down to his place and pick up the check myself.

A couple of weeks later I had a note from Major Lambert: "I see that Mrs. Chapone's *Letters* have rapidly increased in value. Ernest North is willing to let me have them for $1500." Ten years later I noticed that this was still one of Mr. North's prize possessions.

The late Luther Livingston is best known today as the editor of the first four volumes of *American Book Prices Current,* issued in four fat quartos. I think of him more as the first bookseller in America whose catalogues gave truly accurate descriptions of the books.

After Mr. Livingston died, Dodd, Mead (whose rare-book business he had run) gave up their extremely swanky store at 35th Street and Fifth Avenue, and moved their publishing offices and the remainder of their rare-book department to 30th Street and Fourth Avenue. Robert Dodd was in charge of the rare books.

One day my partner, Adolph Stager, and I were doing nothing except wondering where the next dollar was coming from.

"Adolph," I said, "are you going to the Adirondacks this summer?"

"Yes."

"On what?"

"I don't know. Charlie, are you going to Sebago?"

"Of course."

"On what?"

"I don't know. Let's go in and see the old man."

We were on Fourth Avenue, and we went in and asked Mr. Dodd if he had any old junk left.

He scratched his head. "Well, I've got thousands of those wretched pictures that the Society of Iconophiles put out."

(The Society of Iconophiles was a group of amateurs who specialized in reproducing views of old New York. They printed only a hundred of each picture, at ten dollars a copy.)

"How many?" I asked.

Mr. Dodd went into the back of the store, shuffled around, and finally came back to report that he had eighteen hundred.

"How much?"

"Oh, you can have them for a hundred dollars."

"Look here," I said, "you've been trying for years to sell these things, and you can't do it. If the time has actually come when you want to get rid of them, I'll give you thirty-five dollars in real money."

Dodd capitulated.

"All right," I said, "we'll go down to the bank and get the money." The only bank we could think of was the old Provident Loan Society, five blocks down Fourth Avenue, where Stager pawned his ring for fifty dollars. We went back, handed over the majority of our take, and walked off with the eighteen hundred prints in bundles under our arms.

At this time there was a cigar store on 23rd Street where they used to let us leave our packages. On our way down we ran into Herman Sauer, who was not only a great Lincoln scout but one of the most famous print-sellers this country has ever had. His fame rested on himself, not on his store, because he never had a store. He was equally likely to touch you for ten dollars or to flash a roll of a hundred fifties. He had started life as a conductor on the New York Elevated. He once told me that his introduction to the world of art came when he rented a cold-water flat on the lower East Side. Among the rubbish he found a portfolio of old prints. His wife started to throw them away, but Herman said, "No, let me see if I can't get the price of a beer out of these."

He took them to Robert Fridenberg, who offered him one hundred dollars. That was enough to push Herman into the print business.

This particular day I said to him, "Sauer, have you got any money?"

"Well, yes," he admitted grudgingly.

So we went out into the back of the cigar store and undid our bundles. Sauer picked out six hundred prints at $1.50 each, and peeled the cash off the roll in his pocket. As he was leaving with his package, I stepped into a phone booth and called up Evert J. Wendell.

"E.J.," I said, "I've got twelve thousand dollars' worth of Iconophiles pictures, and they're yours for twelve hundred."

"Bully," he said, "but I can't see you. I'm on my way to the grand jury."

"How long'll you be home?"

"Thirty-five minutes."

"I'll be there in ten."

At his house I spread out the pictures on his big grand piano. Mr. Wendell's eyes gleamed.

"Bully, I'll take them. But I haven't a check here."

"Never mind," I said. "Where are you going now?"

"Down on the subway to City Hall."

"Fine, I'll go with you."

Down at City Hall I spent a penny in a stationery store for a blank check and shoved it under Mr. Wendell's nose. He signed, and Stager and I went on our vacations.

Vacations with me are an end, not a means. I believe in taking at least two, and preferably three, months off, pursuing the greatest of game fish, the smallmouthed bass, with no radio and no old books. It takes a very powerful impulse to make me change my mind.

Once Harry Alpern was driving the Everitts to Snowville, New Hampshire, in a new Plymouth. Even on vacation we had to stop for a word with A. J. Huston, the Portland bookseller. Huston told me of an antique dealer in South Portland who had recently bought nearly a ton of old family papers.

Harry is not such a strong character as I am; he was itching to head for South Portland at once.

"No," said I, "to hell with books. We're going fishing."

Then came four days of steady rain. Finally we decided to take our new car and call on Esposito of South Portland as private collectors.

As I stepped out of the car, I was greeted by a large Italian who said, "How do you do, Mr. Everitt. I hope you drop in and see me."

In the back room I found several hundred letters, excellently classified. One lot interested me—a collection of some two hundred letters from a common soldier in New Mexico to his family in Maine. Crude they were, but probably the best actual description of life in New Mexico during the seventies yet known.

During the two hours I was looking over various piles of papers, Esposito kept chattering over my shoulder. First asking me to call him Tony, he told me about his great discoveries and his wealthy clients. Tony was a man of real imagination.

The time finally came to talk money. "How much for this lot, Tony?"

"You know I have only one price, Mr. Everitt." (Sam Dauber's description of "one price" is "the most I can get for it.") "Three hundred."

"Come on," I said to Harry, "time for us to be getting in the car."

Tony seemed a trifle nervous, so I used an old dodge and left my cane in the back room. As I was retrieving the cane, Tony asked me how much I would pay.

I said $150.

His "Yes!" was so loud I wonder if Huston heard him in Exchange Street. Anyway, Tony paid for that vacation.

One of the outstanding old bookstores in Boston for many years was N. J. Bartlett & Co., at 28 Cornhill. Chase of Bartlett's was known and loved by every bookseller in the United States and Great Britain. After his death the store was in charge of Ned Bartlett, who had very little interest in Americana.

Coming down once by train from Little Sebago, we decided to stop over at the Parker House for a couple of nights. I dropped in on Bartlett, who assured me that nothing new in my line had come in for several months. Then, as I was about to leave, he said, "Oh, Mr. Everitt, here's a volume of pamphlets we've had on exhibition. The price is probably too high; we marked it two hundred dollars."

Nothing but seven eighteenth-century New England quarto pamphlets. If Albert W. Johnston looks up his records, he will find he paid for our weeks at Little Sebago.

On one of the days when Herman Sauer had no roll of fifties in his pocket, he came into my store and said, "They're selling off the stuff at the old Ashland House."

This was a hotel at Fourth Avenue and 25th Street, which I suspect may have given its name to the Ashland telephone exchange, and where at all events I had lunch almost daily for some fourteen years. In spite of this fact I had never been above the first floor.

"Everitt, give me fifty dollars," said Sauer. "There's a painting of Number One Broadway in the parlor and I want it."

I handed him $50. After a while Sauer reappeared around the corner, bringing a bill for $250, less deposit of $50. Sauer said he had expected to buy the thing for $35 or $50, but he wanted it anyway. So I gave him another $200, and this time he returned with the painting.

"Give me another two bucks for cab fare," said Sauer. "I want to take this down and show it to Mr. Hoffman."

He vanished in the depths of a horse-drawn cab, and for two hours I heard no more. He came back by Third Avenue El, with eleven cents in cash, and a check for $750 from Mr. Hoffman, who was one of the chief backers of the New York Historical Society. The painting is now one of the Society's most prized possessions. I consider that my share was as easy a $249 as I ever made. It also proves that the more you pay for a thing, the more you can get for it, if that proves anything.

I did not give up lunching at the Ashland House because the place closed; I had broken the habit some time before. The proprietor was a man named Horace Brockway, six feet tall, with whiskers, a high dignitary in the Metropolitan Life Insurance Company. A group of book people that included, among others, Samuel Hopkins Adams, Ray Stannard Baker, John Phillips, the editor, and Lincoln Steffens had presumptive rights to a back room where we all used to congregate for lunch. Our favorite dish was steak Bordelaise, which, with two vegetables, cost seventy-five cents. Pie or ice cream was a dime, and coffee was a nickel. This left ten cents for the waiter.

One day Mr. Brockway marched in and said, "Boys, I'm sorry, but I've got to raise the price of the steak to eighty-five cents." We all vanished like leaves before the wind.

Now here is a story that makes no sense, has no moral or conclusion, and could not possibly be true. Nevertheless it happened to me.

A perfect stranger came into my store on 23rd Street and said, "Would you be interested in a copy of Horsmanden's *Journal of the Negro Plot in New York?*"

This is an extremely rare book on a plot that was hatched in the 1740's. To make conversation, I said, "Have you got the half title?"

"This is one of the three copies that has it," said the stranger.

"How much do you want for it?" I asked.

"Two hundred dollars."

"I'd be very glad indeed to see it."

"I'll be in here at ten o'clock tomorrow morning."

I had approximately three dollars in the bank, so I called up Lathrop Harper, the most learned of all dealers in Americana. I told him my trouble, and he promised to be on hand at ten o'clock with money in his pocket. At ten o'clock a carriage and pair drew up in front of the store, and our stranger got out, carrying a quarto volume. We looked it over, found it exactly as described, and Harper forked over two hundred dollars.

The stranger started for the door, then turned and said, "By the way, here's a list of some other books I have."

Harper's and my hair stood on end. There were seven books of the most fabulous rarity—the first New York City Directory and six other items equally choice.

"I suppose you'd like my name and address," said the stranger. "Here." He wrote them down. "I can't come back tomorrow, but I'll be here the day after."

We never saw him again.

I sent a man up to the address, hoping for better luck than I had any expectation of.

It was a vacant lot.

Julia Marlowe had a collection of several hundred books relating to the stage. Since practically everyone in the theater was at least a little in love with her, nearly all the books bore long, intimate presentation inscriptions from the authors. The collection thus gave rather a portrait of a great actress. Sam Dauber paid her quite a handsome sum for the books.

When we opened up the cartons in the store, all the flyleaves with inscriptions were gone.

Just as Sam and I were discussing our plight, Julia Marlowe's husband, E. H. Sothern, walked in. He was just as embarrassed as we.

He told us that when he saw Julia starting to tear out fly-leaves, he protested that it wasn't fair or honest. Then, to Sam: "You may not know it, but sometimes Julia is not amenable to reason."

We must still have looked glum.

"Which would you rather?" asked Sothern. "Have me refund your money, or take a thousand of my bookplates for the drama books you have in the store?"

Julia Marlowe was a great actress; she was married to a great gentleman.

I hate stamps, but probably I shouldn't; they don't seem to owe me anything. One day I dropped in at an auction on University Place, where a collection of 3600 volumes about stamp collecting – stamp catalogues, stamp magazines, and so forth – was on the block. I saw half the stamp sharpshooters in New York in the audience. For such keen competitors, they looked awfully friendly, and there was a constant buzz of conversation among them.

Finally one of them reluctantly said, "A hundred dollars."

Always ready to make trouble, I said, "Five hundred!"

At this point Walter Scott, of Scott and O'Shaughnessy, came over and sat down beside me. "Charlie, what are you butting in for? It's worth a hundred dollars for you to sit down and shut up."

"Why, Walter, I didn't know it was against the law for anyone to bid on books at an auction."

I finally bought the lot for nine hundred dollars.

Little as I know about stamps, there are some twenty volumes that I have heard of. It struck me as very curious indeed that not one of these titles was in the collection.

I went back to University Place. "Isidore," I said to the auctioneer, "there didn't happen to be a box missing from that lot of stamp books I bought, did there?"

Isidore's expression of surprise was masterly. "Now you mention it, Charlie, I believe there was one box got left down cellar."

"All right, what are you going to do about it?"

"Oh, I'll take five hundred dollars for it."

"Now, Isidore," I said, "I know you don't want any checks. I'll give you two hundred dollars in nice dirty ten-dollar bills, or else. . . ."

"All right," said Isidore.

The next thing was a visit from Walter Scott. "Can I pick out a few books?" he asked innocently.

"No, Walter, you cannot. I don't know enough about them." Walter departed, shaking his head.

Finally he got to the point of asking what I would take for the lot. I said $3500.

"We'll have to have a meeting."

He came back with the decision: "The best we can do is twenty-two hundred."

"Don't bother me; I told you my price was thirty-five hundred."

Finally he came back: "This is our last word. The very best we can do is twenty-eight hundred."

"Walter," I said, "this is your last chance: thirty-five hundred. Yes or no?"

He allowed they couldn't do it, and departed. So I spent about ten dollars on an elaborate night letter to Wallace Cathcart. He came to town the next day and looked over the collection. They all had green morocco backs, to delight the heart of any librarian. Wallace made no demur at $3500, and since the bindings alone had cost $10,000, I guess the Western Reserve Historical Society had something of a bargain at that.

One of my great pals at the Museum of the American Indian was George Pepper, who collected and cross-indexed pamphlets and ephemeral material on American Indian arts (which I approved of), and stamps (which I did not). He also had a private collection of Indian books, which I approved of more than anything. On his deathbed he said to his wife, "Have Charlie sell my stuff. If I were alive, I could get five hundred dollars for the stamps, but Charlie doesn't know anything about them, so you mustn't expect him to get more than a couple of hundred." Conscious of my ignorance of stamps, I called in three different stamp dealers. Oddly enough, each one offered $160 for his choice of the stamps. I chased them all out.

Then I ran into Walter Scott, the auctioneer, who was a very successful seller of stamps to collectors. "Got a couple of hours, Walter?"

He said sure.

On our way up town in a taxi, I explained that this was not a commercial transaction; I meant to give every cent I took to Mrs. Pepper.

My estimate of time was more than generous. Within thirty minutes Walter said, "There are just a few of these that I can use. They're worth a thousand dollars to me, and Mrs. Pepper can keep the rest."

Some months later I asked Walter if he had got out all right on the Pepper stamps.

"Oh, not too bad – I cleared six hundred dollars."

Then I thought of the other jokers with their $160, and

renewed my resolution never to look at another stamp.

Next came the problem of the classified and indexed pamphlets that Pepper had housed at the Museum of the American Indian.

I managed to get hold of William Gates at the moment when he was librarian of Tulane University. "Bill," I said, as we rode up town, "I'm about to sell you twenty-five dollars' worth of merchandise for a thousand dollars. You are one of about half-a-dozen people in the country that would even know what I'm talking about."

He looked over the collection rather quickly and said, "I see what you mean. Send them down to Tulane."

I said, "Bill, there's a string attached to this. George Pepper spent something like seven years indexing this stuff. If you buy it, you've got to keep it in a separate alcove, and hang a big picture of George over it."

"Glad to," said Bill.

He kept his word. And no sooner was he gone from Tulane than his successor issued a mimeographed catalogue offering most of the Pepper material to the firstcomer at twenty-five cents a pamphlet.

My partner for eighteen years was Adolph Stager. At the start of our association we were lucky enough to have his father, Solomon Stager, occupying the front part of our store. (This is the man whom Henry Wagner, in his reminiscences, called "an old Jew named Solomon Steiger.")

Solomon Stager came from Austria as a young man. Soon after he arrived, his relatives outfitted him with a peddler's tray, which he stocked with all the combs, shoelaces, and other notions that his entire capital would buy. On his first day in business he was attracted to a large, fenced greensward, where a considerable crowd of people had gathered. He went over to the fence, and the crowd, reaching through the palings, soon emptied his tray. When he went around to the gate in order to collect, he found that his pitch was an insane asylum, and he was without both his capital and his stock. Somehow he recovered enough from this blow to start a grocery, where he worked unremittingly (and successfully) until his son Adolph went into the book business. Then old Solomon came along to help out the boy.

By my time, he had a little department of his own with standard new books, dictionaries, and the like. His best seller and favorite book was a modern reprint of Morgan's *Exposé of Freemasonry.* It sold for thirty-five cents retail. He was out to lunch one day when an eager customer came in. But the customer had only a quarter. I knew that the book cost Mr. Stager seven cents, so I thought I might as well turn over eighteen cents for him anyhow.

Mr. Stager, back from lunch, was aroused to the very core of his being by my dereliction. That book was supposed to sell for thirty-five cents, and not the Almighty himself had any business cutting the price by nearly a third. I was made to feel that I had been an extremely thoughtless young man.

Solomon Stager bore me no grudge, however. It was only a few days later that I went to him and said, "Mr. Stager, could you possibly write me a check for ten thousand dollars?"

"Oh, sure – just a minute."

The ten thousand dollars soon brought us back a profit of $3800. I went to Mr. Stager.

"Here," I said, "we made thirty-eight hundred with that ten thousand of yours; half of it belongs to you."

"Oh, don't talk nonsense. While you had the ten thousand,

I lost eleven dollars and seventy-five cents interest on it, and that's what I want back."

To Henry Wagner, Solomon Stager may have been just an old Jew; to me he was the finest old Jew I have ever known, and there is no higher praise.

When Adolph Stager and I separated years later, I had a little money and decided I would go to Europe and amuse myself for a while. But I used to frequent Dauber & Pine's shop, and one day when I came in, I found spread out on the floor about ten thousand volumes that had belonged to a man named Ferris, one of the early photographers, who had traveled all over the West and had never thrown anything away.

"I wish you'd look this stuff over, Charlie," Sam Dauber said. "It cost practically nothing, and I've had an offer of five hundred."

I poked around for a couple of hours. "Sam, if you'll let me write a catalogue of this stuff, I'll guarantee to get five thousand out of it for you."

"All right. Why don't you move your desk in here and do it?"

I spent about five weeks writing and printing the catalogue. When the dust had cleared away, the take was $7200. "You aren't doing anything anyhow," Sam said. "Why don't you handle our Americana on commission, and take any kind of drawing account you want?"

So I came in to look things over, and wound up spending every day of the next seven years at Dauber & Pine's.

I am stunned to discover, on counting up, that it is twenty-five years since I have been in Italy. When I was there with my wife, we had a standing agreement that I would spend the mornings doing junk shops, meet her for lunch at one o'clock, and put in the afternoon doing art galleries. One morning in Florence I went to see Otto Lange, a German who had worked in America, and who usually had a good lot of Americana. I spent the morning picking out odds and ends. He saved his heavy artillery for the last. With something of a flourish he produced a North Carolina pamphlet of which the only known copy was in the John Carter Brown library; and the Brown copy had no map.

Lange's was tagged two hundred dollars.

"Why the price, Lange?" I asked, trying to act hard-bitten.

"It's the only known copy with a map," said Lange calmly.

I shelled out.

When I met Mrs. Everitt for lunch, I announced, "I've just paid the expenses of our trip with something I have in my pocket."

"I don't care anything about that," said she. "It's twenty minutes after one."

For more than two decades the greatest collector of Long Island material was my friend and good customer Orville Ackerley. One day he brought in a man whom he introduced as an authority on Long Island history and one of the coming great collectors, whom we'll call James Lacy. Lacy was the vice-president of a large food company.

Lacy bought steadily from me for two or three years, and then stopped coming. The Hearst papers were full of his misadventures, and I learned by the ever-ready grapevine that he owed money all over town.

There was a hiatus of four years. Then Lacy came into the store, looking rather uncertain of his welcome. "You know what a damned fool I've been," he said, "but I'm trying to get straightened out. Though I have no great amount of money, I get a fair income, and I still can't give up my dream of forming a great Long Island collection. If you're willing, I'd like to go on buying books from you."

"Jim," I said, "you can always buy anything from me that you have money to pay for."

He came in almost weekly for some time, paying probably twenty-five dollars a week in cash for what he found on my shelves.

Then I was going to London, and he asked me if I would try to pick him up a copy of *Simcoe's Journal* under five hundred dollars.

I found and brought back a beauty for $400. When he came in, I showed him the bill, and said he could have the book for $450.

He reached in his pocket, then drew his hand out empty. "Oh, hell, I'll mail you a check tonight when I get home."

The check has not yet arrived, but I soon learned that he had sold *Simcoe* the next morning to a New Jersey dealer for a hundred dollars.

The memory of Jim Lacy has always made me rather unhappy. Another experience cost me nearly as much money, but somehow left a far better taste. One of the most famous and sought-after books of North Carolina history is Draper's book on the battle of King's Mountain. I don't know why the battle of King's Mountain is suddenly more important than Yorktown or Ticonderoga, but everyone whose ancestor fought there has to have a copy of the book. Some two decades ago the State of North Carolina announced a big historical celebration. I thought this was an appropriate time for Dauber & Pine to issue a reprint of Draper. A friend of Sam Dauber's offered to manufacture five hundred copies of the book by offset lithography for $850.

The friend forgot to write this down, and the bill, when it arrived, read $1250. We had been less cautious and had announced in print a retail price of $7.50, which in those post-1929 days we could not blithely increase. At all events, the North Carolina newspapers gave us a splendid send-off; we were benefactors to every lover of North Carolina history. The publicity soon brought me a letter from a man who peddled books throughout North Carolina. He asked my wholesale price for twenty-five copies.

I told him four-fifty a copy. He wrote back, "My credit is no good around here; in fact, I am a well-known faker, and you must never ship me anything until my checks have cleared the bank, because they sometimes come back. I hope you will let me have twenty-five copies of your book."

I wrote that I would; he sent me a check for $112.50; when the bank reported that the check had cleared, I shipped twenty-five Drapers.

The same thing happened three more times, which took a certain amount of time because each check was some ten days going through the clearing process. Finally he ordered a hundred copies, with a check for $450. I had noticed that the checks always took either nine or ten days to clear. This time I waited ten days without calling the bank, then thought what the hell, and shipped the books.

They were hardly at the express office when I found that the check was rubber. His perfect timing has always mystified me.

About thirty or thirty-five years ago there was a flutter in the book trade at the appearance of a prosperous new customer for material on the Indians. When he came to see me, he introduced himself as Howard Bible, adding that he was a barrister admitted to practice in both England and Canada. I soon found out that he knew a lot about Indian material, quite a bit of which I sold to him.

For all the law degrees he boasted of, he made his living selling advertising material to banks.

Then for about five years there was one of the complete silences that seem to descend periodically on some of my customers.

One day my wife and I were standing in the hot sun at St. James's Park, waiting for a parade to begin. There is a low, one-story building fronting the park, on the roof of which the aristocracy congregate for such occasions. We had been standing for an hour or more and were about ready to sit down somewhere, when whom should I see but Howard Bible, complete with frock coat, top hat, and yellow gloves, on the rooftop among the nobility and gentry.

I managed to catch his eye, waved my cane, and was gratified to have him beckon us over. We joined him in the sanctum; flunkies produced chairs. Bible introduced us around to Lord This and Lady That.

Thinking to return the compliment and show my gratitude for a place to sit down, I suggested lunch the next day at the Horseshoe. He accepted with an alacrity that did not altogether match his frock coat.

After lunch he asked where I was going, and I said I had run out of cash and was going to replenish my supply at the American Express Company. He said he would walk me down there.

When I emerged into the Haymarket, buttoning down my pockets over fifty pounds, Bible said, "Charlie, you've simply got to let me have thirty-five pounds. My wife and I haven't been eating, and we're a month behind on our rent."

What could I do but fork over? My wife kidded me about it all the way back across the Atlantic.

I had not been at home very long when the vice-president of a downtown trust company telephoned and asked if I bought books about Indians. He wanted me to come down at eleven the next morning and inspect a collection they had.

He took me up to a high floor in the bank's skyscraper and solemnly flung open the door upon serried ranks of old friends – the culls of Howard Bible's collection. Howard had put all the real rarities in storage in Washington; these were the everyday, reading books.

"Would you be interested in buying these?" the banker asked.

"How badly are you stuck?" I retorted.

He flushed. "What do you mean, stuck?"

"Well, I know every book in this room belongs to Howard Bible, and they must be in your hands for some reason."

"Well, we have a loan to him of fifteen thousand."

I poked around a little, just to make sure, and said, "I'll give you fifteen hundred."

The vice-president was quite put out. He went over and pulled off the shelf a set of Catlin's *Indians* in the Grant reprint. "But we have the owner's appraisal of forty thousand for the collection, and he values this one item at three hundred."

"That's fine," I said. "But all the same, I have a set listed in my catalogue for seven dollars and a half."

There was some more back-chat, which finally ended with my writing out a check for $1500. As I was leaving the bank skyscraper, I told myself that Howard no longer owed me thirty-five pounds. (This was just as well, because some years afterward, in the course of a fair-sized transaction, he told me the same thing himself.)

One of the most interesting issues of the *National Geographic Magazine,* and in fact quite a collector's item by now, is the number on Flags of the World, by Captain "Brick" McCandless, U.S.N.

With the exception of Frank Dobie, Brick is the best storyteller I have ever known. There were six of us in our store on 34th Street one day, fondly contemplating two bottles of bourbon and two bottles of Scotch, when Brick McCandless walked in. We had a lounging room upstairs, to which we retired, with an anticipatory alcoholic gleam in our eyes. Before the corks were drawn, I happened to ask Brick something about his work on the flag number of the *National Geographic.*

He told us for three hours; and for three hours nobody pulled a cork.

Brick's son was a hero of World War II, but by that time he was an old story to me. Brick told us about the time when he was in command of a flotilla of three vessels, and put into Istanbul. Young McCandless, then aged ten or eleven, was aboard, and Brick took him for a walk through the town. A curious set of dishes caught Brick's eye, and he remarked casually, "I wish I had enough money to buy those and take them home to Mother."

When the announced hour for weighing anchor came, young McCandless was "absent without leave." The irate father and commander paced the quarterdeck for about two hours before his young hopeful was discovered on the dock followed by two burly Turks carrying bundles.

The flotilla shoved off in hot haste, and McCandless *père*

called his offspring to account. The boy was surprised and hurt at the excitement.

"But Father, you said you wanted to take those dishes to Mother, only you didn't have enough money. Well, I went into the place, and they wanted seven-fifty for the dishes, but I said I only had three dollars, so they sold them. I had them bring them along, didn't I?"

The next stop on Brick's cruise was Naples. Many of his crew being Catholic, he thought they would appreciate the opportunity of an audience with the Pope. He arranged it for the whole crew. His Holiness received them most amiably, and when the audience was over, asked if they would not like to see the Vatican Library. The sailors were probably not too much interested, but Brick, being a book collector, thought it was the chance of a lifetime, and said so. The American visitors were escorted through some outlying rooms with a few thousand volumes of the complete works of Carlo Goldoni. Their further progress was barred by an iron gate, under the protection of a Swiss Guard.

"So far and no further," said the guard, or gestures to that effect.

"Hey, what is this?" Brick expostulated. "His Holiness told us we could see the Vatican Library."

The Swiss Guard declined to lift his halberd.

"All right," said Brick, "we're going back and take this up with His Holiness." There was a great flutter among the lackeys. No one had ever heard of two successive audiences with the Pope. But the United States Navy was as immovable as the Swiss Guard. Finally Brick actually penetrated once more to His Holiness. "Holy Father," said Brick, "it was my understanding that we were to see the Vatican Library, but some man at the gate declines to let us through."

The Pope smiled. "My son, perhaps Napoleon gave us bad habits. Since he looted the library, no man in uniform has been allowed to set foot within the inner gate. But for you I shall be glad to break a rule that is hardly more than a hundred years old." And he scribbled an order that turned Brick and his bluejackets loose at will throughout the Vatican Library.

The next stop was Spain. Brick's great ambition there was to photograph for his flag book the flag of the Invincible Armada. He had taken the precaution of getting high-powered letters from the President and other dignitaries to the King of Spain.

These produced no results whatever. He might just as well have been applying to marry the Infanta.

"But Brick," I objected, "I saw the Armada flag in your book."

"Oh, sure," he said. "I just went to the Alhambra and slipped the custodian two bits."

Stone & Kimball were two Harvard boys who started the most spectacular and literary publishing house of the turn of the nineteenth century. They brought a breath of fresh air into the publishing business, were extravagantly respected and admired by all the advance guard, and folded up within a few years because they could never seem to get more than $1.50 for books that cost them $2.50 to print and bind. Today they are among the very, very few publishing houses whose imprints are collected for the publisher's name quite aside from the authorship.

Peter Stammer, the eccentric and rough-tongued Fourth Avenue bookseller, paid a dollar a barrel for thirty-one barrels of Stone & Kimball's correspondence. I spent days going over the haul — letters from Stevenson, letters from Shaw, letters from every author you ever heard of, and a lot you never did.

I gave Stammer some twelve hundred dollars for the thing I wanted, but there was one lot he flatly refused to sell. These were letters from Fiona Macleod, the "young Scottish romantic authoress." Fiona Macleod was a great sensation of the nineties, and it gradually began to be suspected that she was a figment of the imagination of an obscure middle-aged author named William Sharp. The letters in the Stone & Kimball papers were the first definite proof that this suspicion was correct.

Stammer, who could be charming to his friends, would let me have nearly anything I wanted; but about Fiona Macleod he remained obdurate. Finally E. D. Brooks, a collector-bookseller in Minnesota whose one interest in life was the new authors of the nineties, told me he had to have the Fiona Macleod letters, come what might. After he had told me this two or three times, I went down to Stammer and said, "Look here, you're going to sell me those Fiona Macleod letters, and I'm not going to pay you over a hundred dollars. Five years hence they won't be worth a nickel, so you might as well get out while the getting is good."

After considerable back-chat, I gave him the hundred dollars and sold the letters to Brooks at the same figure.

(Mr. Brooks died soon afterward and not a word has been heard of his collection since.)

When Alfred Potter was librarian at the Harvard College Library, I was one of two booksellers who had free access to the library duplicate room, and whose appraisals he accepted without question. The other dealer, being a Bostonian, seldom went near the place. (I never go to the New York Public any more, either.) After Mr. Potter retired, the library hired a young expert to price the duplicates for sale to dealers. One day when I was in there, I saw a very nice set of Audubon's *Birds of America* in the 1840–44 edition, priced at three hundred dollars. This was just about the retail price, so I was in no great hurry to buy.

Then I noticed on the next shelf two cheaply rebound cloth volumes marked *Cabinet of Natural History*, Vols. I and II. I thought this might help to pay my fare home to New York, so I said to the young man, "I see you have this tagged at ten dollars. If you'll throw it in with the Audubon, I'll give you three hundred for both."

He did so. Then the *Cabinet of Natural History* sat on my shelves for several weeks in New York. It is one of the rarest of all American sporting items; it ran through two complete volumes, and the publisher went broke in the middle of volume three. So of course every bookseller who saw my set immediately yelled, "Where's the third volume?"

One day when I was really hard up for something to do, I started to collate the set, to see if at least all the plates were there in the volumes I had.

Not only were they all there, but the fragmentary volume three was bound in at the back of volume two. When I finally sold the set to a leading dealer in sporting books, I could have shown a slight profit even if I had given the Audubon away.

Sprinkled over the smaller towns of England are quite a lot of bookstores where, if you are lucky enough to beat the London dealers, you can do all right. For instance, my partner Sam Dauber once acquired a great collection of drawings and paintings by Randolph Caldecott, the illustrator of children's books, for fifty pounds. The packing and shipping cost almost as much again as the collection itself. When the things arrived, I promptly called up Mr. Potter, because Harvard takes pride in its collection of juvenile illustrators. He asked if he could have the lot on approval, and I sent them right up.

Shortly afterward he telephoned: "I don't know what you want for this collection, but we'd like to make a choice out of the stuff. Some of the things interest us more than others. I have a friend of the library here who is willing to contribute seven hundred and fifty dollars for the stuff we choose."

"No, Mr. Potter," I said, "that collection is unique, and it's not to be broken up. I know it's worth a great many times that, but to keep it from being dispersed, you can have the whole thing for seven hundred and fifty."

The next I heard from Potter was a letter containing a check for a thousand dollars. "My friend and I heartily agree that it would be a crime to break up the collection, and we would be deeply ashamed to pay you less than a thousand dollars for it."

One of my frequent hangouts was the Fifth Avenue Gallery, which of course was on Fourth Avenue at 24th Street, and was run by a man named Norman. You never knew what you would find there, or whom, either.

Once they announced a sale of Napoleonana. This is a subject about which I care nothing, and know less. Anyway, I went to the sale. There must have been ten thousand items out of the one or two or three hundred thousand in existence bearing on Napoleon. As I came in, they were selling off fifty-one volumes of a newspaper published during Napoleon's time. All I knew about the newspaper was that it had been reprinted a number of times, and (from the date) that this was the original edition. For no reason at all I joined in the bidding, and carried off the prize at fifty-one dollars (in those days there was a custom sometimes of selling sets by the volume).

After I had it, I did not know what to do with it. Pretty obviously a library was the only possible taker, so I checked up to find out what my various librarian friends held.

I was soon seated at Mr. Potter's desk. "I see you lack this," I said. "What do you know about it?"

"Nothing, except that I've been looking for it for twenty years."

"Well, what's it worth?" I asked.

"I have no idea," said Mr. Potter.

"I think you ought to give me a thousand dollars for it, anyway," I said.

"I don't know anything about book prices," Mr. Potter said, "only I've found that there are some booksellers in the country who don't like to overcharge a person, so I'll take this set."

My price was a perfectly blind guess, but I have since found out by talking to Napoleon collectors that Mr. Potter and I were both right.

On another occasion I wandered into the Fifth Avenue Gallery, and found a great mass of documents concerning Kingston, New York. If there was one, there were four thousand. Most of them were in Dutch. The whole mass was put up as one lot. No other dealers were there. If it had not been for a customer of mine, a man named Smith, from Madison, New Jersey, I could probably have had the whole shebang for ten dollars. Smith pushed me to three hundred.

The next day he telephoned. "I'll take those Kingston documents you bought yesterday," he said.

"What do you mean, take them?"

"Well, you've been buying at auctions for me on a ten per

cent commission for a long time; I figured that makes these worth three hundred and thirty dollars."

"Did you give me any order to buy these?"

"Well, no, but that's always been our arrangement in the past."

"I haven't looked at these yet," I said, "but I can tell you now that 10 per cent on this deal is going to be three thousand dollars."

"I'll never buy a book of you as long as I live," said Smith, and slammed up the phone.

(He never did, either.)

Most of the manuscripts were Dutch, and hence double Dutch to me. I hired a Dutch girl to look them over and note the general subject of each document in pencil at the top.

One of my callers soon afterwards was Dr. Victor Hugo Paltsits, the great scholar from the New York Public Library. He picked up one of my Kingston documents, looked at the penciled heading, and began to laugh. I looked over his shoulder. The note said, "Religious controversy in Kingston."

"What's the matter?" I asked.

"Why, this really is the first set of police regulations for Albany, in the middle of the seventeenth century." Another lot that caught his eye was all the documents concerning the attempt to make Kingston the capital of the United States, an effort that failed by one vote. I let my respect for Dr. Paltsits and his institution run away with my financial judgment when I sold that part of the lot to him. A few months later I would have been overjoyed to buy back those manuscripts at ten times what Dr. Paltsits paid me.

Incidentally, I listed the most important of these manuscripts and sent the list to Dr. James Wyer, then State Librarian in New York, who never even bothered to reply.

After I had sold most of the stuff, I picked out a deed that somehow looked interesting. Usually deeds put me to sleep, but for some reason I described this one elaborately, and catalogued it at $35.

Two days after the catalogue went out, a perfect stranger telephoned from Kingston: "Have you still got that deed?"

"Yes."

"All right, I'll telephone my lawyer to bring you in thirty-five dollars right away."

I said, "Don't be nervous; it's yours."

About an hour later a lawyer marched in from down town, laid thirty-five dollars on my desk, and started to remove the deed.

"Hey, what's all the excitement?" I asked. I thought possibly some local celebrity was involved, or a new collector was getting the bug.

"Well, this client of mine has spent forty years trying to clear his title to some land, and this deed gives it to him on a silver platter. It would probably have been cheap for him to pay you thirty-five hundred for it."

I have talked through nearly a whole book about how important it is for a bookseller to know everything. I find I have barely touched on the very considerable cash value of ignorance. A men's clothing trade journal in West 38th Street folded up once, and the receiver asked me to come and look at the office library. There were three huge, ungainly bookcases full of books on men's tailoring, no doubt one of the finest existing collections on the subject.

Too ignorant to be impressed, I grumbled to the receiver, "Oh, I'll give you fifty bucks."

"All right," said the receiver, "but you know you have to remove the bookcases too."

I called up Evert Wendell, who kept a huge loft for just such purposes, and said, "E. J., I've got three great big bookcases over here a couple of blocks from your loft. If you'll pay a truck man to take them away, you can have them."

That disposed of the bookcases, but what to do with the books? There I sat in my store, with two or three thousand volumes, asking myself why the hell I had ever wasted fifty dollars.

Then came a stroke of genius: these were costume books.

I wrote an elaborate description to Wallace Cathcart of the Western Reserve Historical Society, who was very proud of his costume collection, and lured him East.

We finally decided that this unique collection was worth nine hundred dollars to the library if I would pay the freight.

Once when I was in London Bertram Rota phoned to say he had just bought a fine copy of *Logan,* by Major Rogers. Fifteen minutes and two bob in taxi fare took me to Rota's office. I found him embarrassed and distressed. He said that just after he had hung up, he noticed that this copy, fine as it seemed, lacked the half-title. He let me have it, with many apologies, for half price.

I took it to Ernest Zaehnsdorf, and asked him to make me a facsimile half-title.

For my next catalogue I noted, "Fine copy of first edition. Half-title in facsimile."

Lathrop Harper, dropping in, saw my note ready for the printer. He began to laugh harder and harder. "Charlie," he said "*Logan* never did have a half-title."

At last I owned a unique book. The only copy of *Logan* with even a faked half-title.

(Bibliography is such an exact science – so far nobody has

the slightest idea who was the author of *Logan,* "attributed to Major Rogers.")

Nearly everyone except the authorities in charge of the Mark Twain Estate has read or at least heard of Mark Twain's item of facetiae entitled *Conversation at an Elizabethan Breakfast Table,* usually referred to by the short title of *1601.* Some of the sprightlier elements in Mark Twain's regular publishing house struggled for years to get the thing legitimately into print, but never succeeded.

Mark wrote the story, of course, simply to amuse himself. But, being a great craftsman, he sent the manuscript to a Harvard professor to have his Elizabethan English checked. The professor turned out a revised version.

This fact led Merle Johnson and me to think that a variorum edition would be a laudable enterprise.

The first point was to prove that Mark Twain had written *1601.* Everybody knew he had, but when we went through the correspondence, there was not a scrap of writing for evidence.

Finally we tracked down a man in California who, for a hundred dollars, let us reproduce a note from Mark acknowledging his authorship.

(There is a famous, and undoubtedly true, story that has always pleased me: John Hay, the poet diplomat, sent a manuscript copy loaned to him by Mark Twain to a friend in Cleveland. The friend replied that this was the funniest thing he had ever read; he proposed to make a printing of it for distribution among his friends. Hay replied, "Naturally neither Mr. Clemens nor I could dream of permitting you to print this manuscript. If you should do so, however, please send me ten copies.")

Johnson and I produced our variorum edition, to the number of 110 copies. As usually happens in cases like that, we had at least 250 orders beforehand. We filled all we could, and found ourselves – also as usual in such cases – just about swapping dimes in the matter of cost and income. To add insult to injury, neither of us could even keep a copy for ourselves.

A decade later I was walking down St. Martin's Lane, London, when my eye was caught by a large sign: STONEWALL JACKSON, THE CHEAPEST BOOKSTORE IN LONDON. Standing in front of the shop was a lanky Englishman. I accosted him. "How did you get that name?"

"Oh, that's my real name. My parents never heard of any darn Confederate general."

"All right, have you got any Americana?"

He reached behind a counter and said, "Here, how about this?"

It was a copy of the variorum edition of *Conversation at an Elizabethan Breakfast Table.* Stonewall Jackson was both pleased and surprised, but even more surprised than pleased, when I offered him thirty shillings for the book.

After World War I the regular newsboy in front of the Abbotsford Hotel was an ex-soldier. We used to pay him a shilling for a penny paper, and as a result soon heard about his troubles, the worst of which was that on a good day he might clear two shillings. One morning he stopped me and a friend on the street with the remark, "I've got a hot tip for the handicap."

In my experience these tips are the best you can get, so each of us handed him a pound. But when we looked in the papers to see how we had done, we could not find any such horse as the one he had mentioned running in any of the races.

The next day he stopped us with a broad grin and handed us each ten pounds.

"This is fine, old man," I said, "but I couldn't find any such horse running at any of the tracks."

He grinned even more broadly. "Oh, didn't I tell you? This wasn't a horse, it was a dog."

John T. Winterich, a friend and customer of mine, once remarked in the *Saturday Review of Literature* that far too few authors give credit to rare-booksellers for the help they get. Part of the occasion for Winterich's remarks was an anthology whose foreword mentioned my help in compiling it.

As a matter of fact, perhaps one reason why authors do not mention the help they get from booksellers is that not many booksellers make a hobby of helping authors.

Helping authors is quite a difficult branch of bookselling, not – as you might suppose – because authors can't afford to buy really rare books, but because an author never starts looking for a particular title until he needs it to write his next chapter.

Another point is that far more often than early rarities they need sound works of modern scholarship five or six years old. These books almost invariably flop when published; the publisher remainders them for twenty-five or fifty cents, nobody pays any attention, and then suddenly all copies vanish like water soaking into sand.

A friend of mine has been searching ever since the war for a copy of A. J. Liebling's *The Telephone Booth Indians,* which was published during the war, and even reissued in a twenty-five-cent paper reprint. In the time he has spent unsuccessfully hunting for this, I suspect he might have found several copies of Catlin's *Indians of North America.*

I had a fairly close view of the process as shown through a man named Charles Wood, who made a comfortable fortune selling stoves in Dayton, Ohio. He marched into my store one day, a perfect stranger, and said that he thought the existing histories of the Apache Indians were inaccurate, and he wanted to assemble a collection of material that would straighten the story out. In the course of ten years he learned that what he had expected to cost him two or three thousand dollars would run to forty or fifty thousand, but he kept on. Then he died suddenly (two hours before an auction for which he had wired me a lot of big bids). His material, however, instead of being bequeathed to a library, and sold for scrap paper, was shaped by Frank C. Lockwood into a book that superseded all others about the Apache Indians, just as Mr. Wood had intended.

The Macmillan Company published the book, but they sold less than two thousand copies. Naturally, since my office was next door to their building, no Macmillan salesman had ever heard of me. They scuttled to remainder the book – an opportunity I seized upon to sell some three hundred copies. I doubt whether either of the big book wholesalers bought a much larger quantity of the title than that.

Not infrequently I am called in to appraise, instead of buy, a library.

When the president of the Delaware, Lackawanna and Western Railroad, Samuel Sloan, died, I had a phone call from his namesake, a son or nephew. He asked me if I would appraise the library at the house on 38th Street just east of Fifth Avenue. I said I would, for a hundred dollars.

"The fee's not your problem, Everitt," he said. "The books have to be divided among seven elderly ladies, and they'll all be present while you are making the appraisal."

Nevertheless, I went. The seven ladies apparently disliked one another heartily. I suggested that it would be a good idea to give the set of Scott to one lady, the set of Dickens to another, and so on down the line.

Not at all. Each set had to be evenly divided among the legatees.

Here I was the stumbling block: I have never learned how to divide twenty- or thirty-volume sets into seven even parts. Finally I said, "Look, suppose we put all these books in a pile on the floor, and you ladies can walk round and round and each choose one volume at a time."

This worked splendidly until we came to a beautiful set of Audubon. Four volumes were even harder to divide by seven than twenty. So I stepped outside to consult the executor.

"What's this worth?" he asked.

Remembering the number of ladies, I pared down my appraisal by a hundred dollars or so, and said, "Seven thousand dollars."

"All right. I'll keep those, and send them each a thousand dollars." Evidently pleased with my diplomacy, he called again later to ask if I would appraise the books at the country estate up the Hudson.

He had some lumpers ready to carry the books downstairs for me to look at. They consisted entirely of "Delay, Linger, and Wait" reports during Sloan's presidency. My method here was to make a rough guess at the weight of the paper. I appraised the collection at fifteen dollars, added in my railroad fare, and sent a bill for $103.60. This, I'm happy to say, brought me a check and a letter of thanks.

At the other extreme from Samuel Sloan's country library is the collection of Vilhjalmur Stefansson, which was beyond all comparison the longest and also the most interesting appraisal I ever made.

If I simply say that Stef has made the world's greatest collection of material concerning the Arctic and the northern countries, I shall probably give the impression that he has a lot of stories about ships frozen in the ice. Actually the collection covers the entire social, physical, and economic life and history of nearly a third of the globe. Stef has kept himself poor for most of his lifetime by unremitting devotion to those books.

I once heard him say to one of his secretaries, "I've got to go on a trip. Will you cash me a check for two hundred and fifty dollars?"

"But, Mr. Stefansson, we haven't got two hundred and fifty dollars."

"How can that be?"

"Don't you remember that you told me yesterday to pay the back book bills? I drew out twenty-five hundred for that."

I found a shelf of books on falconry, and asked Stef why he had bought them.

"Well," he explained, "in the days when the nobility hunted with falcons, they used the white falcon, which was a royal bird for kings, secular princes, and their opposite numbers in the Church. . . . the white falcon of Iceland and Greenland was so valuable that generally it was not sold but was given as a princely gift, a recognized and proper kind of bribery. Falcons were also used for kingly ransoms."

The contents of the collection are enough to take your breath away, but the real expense, and the real value, comes from the fact that Stef has cross-indexed every page in every volume he owns. You look in his card index under "whales," and you can turn to the right page in more than three hundred different books or magazines. I am sure this indexing has cost more than the books did.

(The New York Public Library used to figure that it cost them $2.50 to shelve any book that was given to them free. And I remember once seeing Alfred Potter at the Harvard Library tell an accession clerk to order the entire contents of some German catalogue. This was just after World War I, during the German inflation, but even so I was somewhat startled. "Why," said Potter, "it's cheaper to buy them than to check the catalogue and see if we have them.")

Stef's collection has some thousands of magazines, normally worth a nickel apiece, each containing some sort of article on the north. On the strength of the indexing, I decided arbitrarily that each magazine was going to be worth a dollar.

Occasionally Stef would come in and look over my shoulder while I was at work. I put down two little German books on whaling at $250. "Charlie, that's ridiculous," he objected. "I paid fifty cents apiece for them."

"All right, can I have them for three hundred?"

"Oh, I can't win an argument with you! Get on with your work."

I look back on this job with considerable satisfaction, because I do not think there are three other people alive who could have done the job so well. Even so, I would have been utterly lost without Stef's wife Evelyn, whose knowledge of languages made it possible for me to tell what I was doing.

About every half-hour during the twenty-two days I spent on the appraisal, I was shocked by the discovery of some item quite unknown to bibliographers. I remember one twenty-four-page pamphlet in Latin, printed in Germany, which was undoubtedly the first doctoral dissertation on the Northwest

Passage. Then again there was a Russian atlas, one of the rarest in the world. Stef's copy, however, was accompanied by a second volume showing sailing routes. This kind of thing kept me in a state of perpetual amazement.

I don't like to mention my final, total appraisal, partly because I am afraid it may be much too low. I have always considered it an axiom that any reasonably good collection is worth at least 20 per cent more than its component parts, but Stef's collection may easily be worth twice as much.

Speaking of Stef and the Arctic reminds me of two stories having not the slightest connection with books.

One of the best loved members of the Explorers' Club was Captain Bob Bartlett, an uneducated old Nova Scotiaman who was nearly the best lecturer I have ever heard. I have listened to the same lecture five successive times with great enjoyment.

Nearly any explorer will tell you that the Explorers' Club Medal is the distinction he would most like in all the world. Very few of them have ever been given. Bob Bartlett was to have one, and in honor of the occasion they held a big banquet at the McAlpin Hotel.

Someone got up and made a conventional, rather pallid, presentation address.

When Bob stood up to reply, the tears were streaming down his face. "All I can say," he managed to choke out, "is, you're a goddamned fine bunch of fellows!"

Once Bob was supposed to give a lecture at the Kent School, presided over by the famous and extremely saintly Father Sill. Two or three friends and I took Bob aside beforehand and said, "Look, Bob, this is one time when you *cannot* swear. You just can't do it."

I heard later from a faculty wife who questioned her two small boys about the lecture.

"Yes," said one of the boys, "it was very interesting, but Captain Bartlett swore."

"Oh, I don't think he'd do that, surely."

"Yes, he did too. When Father Sill came in in his robes, I heard Captain Bartlett say, 'Jesus Christ!' "

Looking back over five decades, I find the net result is a few hundred old books and glorious memories. When I stop to wonder about the money that poured through my hands, I guess it must have been the landlords and the printers and the promising friends that took it.

The best I can do is let Frank Dobie write my epilogue:

> We all met in your office at Dauber & Pine's in March, 1931 – Dellenbaugh, Stefansson, Hodge, and myself. I don't recollect so much of the conversation, but the geniality and warmth of the company, led by our host, remains with me so vividly that my spirits rise now remembering it. . . .
>
> Never was a merrier host than you, Charlie. When I read 'Master Francis Beaumont's letter to Ben Jonson,' I think of that company.
>
> What things have we seen
> Done at the Mermaid! heard words that have been
> So nimble and so full of subtle flame,
> As if that every one from whence they came,
> Had meant to put his whole wit in a jest
> And had resolved to live a fool the rest
> Of his dull life . . .
> And, when we were gone
> We left an air behind us, which alone
> Was able to make the next two companies
> Right witty.
>
> Frank.